Warning signs

STOP 100 yds
Distance to STOP sign ahead

Cross roads

Roundabout

T junction

Staggered junction

GIVE WAY 50 yds
Distance to GIVE WAY sign ahead

Side road

REDUCE SPEED NOW
Plate below some signs

Sharp deviation of route to left (or right if chevrons reversed)

Bend to right (or left if symbol reversed)

Double bend first to left (may be reversed)

Series of bends

Two-way traffic straight ahead

Two-way traffic crosses one-way road

Traffic merges from left

Traffic joins from right

Road narrows on offside (nearside if symbol reversed)

Road narrows on both sides

Dual carriageway ends

Steep hill downwards
1:10

Steep hill upwards
1:6

Children

Single file traffic
Single file in each direction

Pedestrian crossing

Traffic signals

Hump bridge

Uneven road

School
Plate with CHILDREN sign at a school

Single track road
Road wide enough for only one line of traffic

Road works

Change to opposite carriageway (may be reversed)

Right-hand lane closed (symbols may be varied)

Slippery road

Patrol 200 yds
Plate with CHILDREN sign near school crossing patrol

Level crossing with automatic half-barriers ahead

Level crossing with other barrier or gate ahead

Level crossing without gate or barrier ahead

Location of level crossing without gate or barrier

'Count-down' markers approaching concealed level crossing

DRIVING TODAY
THE B.S.M. WAY

DRIVING TODAY
The B.S.M. Way

TOM WISDOM

and

RONALD PRIESTLEY

Illustrations by Lionel Burrell

PETER DAVIES : LONDON

Peter Davies Ltd
15 Queen Street, Mayfair, London W1X 8BE
LONDON · MELBOURNE · TORONTO
JOHANNESBURG · AUCKLAND

432 19355 3

First published 1963
Reprinted twelve times
This edition 1972

British School of Motoring
Head Office: 102 Sydney Street, London SW3
Tel.: 01-352 1014

Filmset and Printed Offset Litho in Great Britain by
Cox & Wyman Ltd, London, Fakenham and Reading

Contents

List of Diagrams

Foreword

to the New Edition of B.S.M.'s Driving Manual

by Miss Denise McCann, M.I.M.I.,
Chairman and Managing Director of
The British School of Motoring

It gives me considerable pleasure to write a Foreword to this new edition of B.S.M.'s Driving Manual which was first published in 1963.

There is little I can add to what I wrote nearly ten years ago, except to say that the new edition has been thoroughly brought up to date and that the book has proved a great success, in its various reprints, in helping drivers not only to pass the driving test but to become safe and, I hope, happy motorists.

There are more cars to the square mile on Britain's roads than on those of any other motor-minded country in the world. This sobering thought underlines the vital necessity for us to be able to drive safely and well—it is literally a matter of life and death for all road users.

That is why this book can do nothing but good and why the British School of Motoring, the world's biggest driving school, with more than half a century of experience behind it, is glad to be associated with it.

Written by Tom Wisdom and Ronald Priestley, both founder members of the exclusive High Performance Club, it takes as its basis the proved training principles of the B.S.M. to give the reader the background, method and detail, combined with the authors' acknowledged skill, for the promotion of safe, skilful driving.

The authors are both motorists of world-wide repute.

Tom Wisdom has achieved fame in three fields: as a racing and rally driver, author and journalist. His history of driving achievements is too long to record in detail in this foreword, but includes successes in such races as the Portuguese Grand Prix, Monaco Grand Prix, Le Mans 24-hours Race and the Targa Florio (Sicily). He won the Gran Turismo Class three times in the Mille Miglia; lowered records with Captain George Eyston and the late John Cobb; won four Alpine Cups in International Alpine Trials; has competed in 25 consecutive Monte Carlo Rallies; was awarded the E.R.A. Trophy for Best British Performance in Motor Races Abroad, 1949, and in 1961 received the Lord Rootes Gold Cup for Outstanding Achievement of the Year by a member of the Guild of Motoring Writers (of which he is a founder member) for his drive in the East African Safari Rally. Even during the writing of this book he took part in three famous events—the Monte Carlo Rally, the East African Safari Rally and the Alpine Trial.

Ronald Priestley was for many years Senior Instructor of the Essex Police Advanced Wing Driving School. He then became Chief Instructor to the British School of Motoring, supervising the country's only training school for instructors, and he is now Consultant on instruction given throughout the United Kingdom and Europe by the B.S.M. He is regularly called upon for radio and television broadcasts and is an authority on safe driving. He has travelled extensively in America and on the Continent studying road safety methods.

This is a book written by experts. I feel sure no single driver among my acquaintances—and through my job I know more motorists than most people—who will not benefit from reading it.

1

Introduction

Driving today is a serious business.

It was not always so. In the beginning it was an adventure, a sport for the privileged few. In 1900 there were only 20,000 vehicles on the roads of Britain; in terms of mileage those roads were almost as long as they are now, so the car and driver of those early days of the twentieth century had plenty of space in which to manoeuvre. Roads have, of course, been improved. They have been widened, properly surfaced and lighted, made safer by dual carriageways and by-passes. Latterly motorways have been and are being built to replace the narrow, winding tracks that still form the basis of our road system.

As the motor car improved and became more reliable it began to take its place in the social life of the nation, although not without a bitter struggle did it finally replace the horse, behind whose broad beam were concealed powerful vested interests. Typical of the general reaction of the period was this extract from the *Cab Trade Record* in 1900:

"The racing and violence of pace of motor cars which *has* now become a feature of the London streets is one of the most serious outrages upon public safety that has been known for many a year. Why the police authorities permit it is a marvel. Probably they will do nothing until the Chief Commissioner or the Home Secretary has been run over and crushed to death. We look forward with great dread to what may happen in the autumn or winter with slippery streets and benumbed horses and drivers. It is clear that if drivers of cabs are to be at the mercy of these

ugly and death dealing machines without the police interfering
with their insane rushes and jumps and starts and sudden pullings
up, etc."

Despite such diatribes the motor car prospered. Public
transport vehicles joined the private car on the roads; light
delivery vans and larger load-carrying vehicles were seen in
ever increasing numbers. These latter brought into being
another class of motorist, one who drove for his livelihood
rather than for the sheer pleasure of the undertaking.

With more and more vehicles on the road accidents
increased. In 1930 the Road Traffic Act was passed: a Highway Code was authorized, a speed limit for commercial
vehicles imposed, and third party insurance for all vehicles
was made compulsory.

In 1935 three million vehicles were in use and there were
250,000 accidents involving death and injury. In an effort to
check these figures a 30 m.p.h. speed limit was enforced in
built-up areas and driving tests were introduced, tests which,
in their basic essentials, remain the same today.

Twenty-five years later in 1960 the total number of vehicles
on our roads exceeded nine million, three times as many as in
1935, yet accidents involving death and injury, instead of
rising in proportion to *three* times 250,000, rose to a total of
275,000. Lest these figures should cause complacency it is
interesting to quote from a paper read at the International
Road Safety Congress at Nice in 1960 by Brigadier R. F. E.
Stoney, then Director-General of the Royal Society for
Prevention of Accidents (RoSPA). He regarded casualty/
vehicle ratios as tending to paint too rosy a picture and had
this to say:

"We must admit that the numbers killed on our roads today
are much the same as pre-war, and the number of injured up very
considerably. We, therefore, prefer to adopt a more realistic
attitude, one we can use to see how we rate in relation to other

countries with like problems, the ratio of road deaths per 100,000 population. Here in spite of the steeply rising number of vehicles and, more significantly, of new drivers in all age groups, on our overcrowded roads, the deaths population ratio has barely risen at all and is still below the pre-war figure. When we compare our ratio with that of the U.S.A. and heavily motorised European countries we find that only Belgium and Norway have a better record to show and some indeed are twice as bad as we."

What has all this to do with my learning to drive? you may ask. The short answer is, everything. *To drive well is to drive safely*. There is a world of difference between the good driver and the one who merely controls a car.

To explain the controls and instruct you in the handling of them is the object of this book, but we shall have failed in our object if we do not convince you that care and concentration and a regard for others on the road is every bit as important as any other aspect of driving. Over the years the operations involved in driving a car have been simplified enormously; the difficulties lie in the relationship between *you* and *your* car and the *other* man in *his* car.

Much of this will be learned from experience, but first it must be taught, and taught according to the rules which are set out in the Highway Code.

It is best to learn to drive when young, when the mind is alert and more easily adaptable and receptive to new ideas. A provisional licence to drive a car can be obtained at the age of 17 years. This is the first essential step towards the acquisition of a full driving licence. The second is a series of lessons to enable you to pass the test.

It is of the utmost importance to approach this step in the correct frame of mind. Do not be "test-conscious". Do not think of your tuition as the necessary preliminaries to passing the test but rather *concentrate upon learning to drive*—then the test will take care of itself. Experience has proved that there are few people who cannot succeed in passing the driving test.

We have stated that it is best to learn to drive when young; this is not to say that one cannot do so much later in life. Indeed the learner driver of, say, 40 years of age, although lacking the adaptability of youth, often brings a more relaxed and mature approach to the task in the form of tolerance and self discipline which the young have still to achieve.

How long will it take me to learn to drive? This is the question every novice asks of his, or her instructor, and it is one that is almost impossible to answer. So much depends upon the individual and his, or her aptitude for driving. As a rough guide it is reasonable to assume that you will need one hour of tuition for each year of your life, thus an 18-year-old should be driving well enough to pass the test after 18 hours; but it could equally be 16 hours, or even 22, it just depends. The question remains particularly difficult because it almost invariably implies another vital, but unspoken query, "how much will it cost me to learn to drive?" The impossibility of giving a firm answer to this has left the driving schools open to the charge that they are in business merely to siphon off your surplus cash in return for as many lessons as they think you will stand for.

Nothing could be farther from the truth. The reputable driving school can be likened to any other manufacturing business where the raw materials go in one end, are processed within the factory as efficiently and cheaply as they can be to certain set specifications, to emerge in due course as a finished product. Whether this be a cake of soap or a good driver, a successful organization depends upon a high turnover and the goodwill engendered by the production of high-quality merchandise.

In the authors' view and in that of those who really understand how important driving tuition is, professional teaching is essential. After all if you need a tooth out you don't go to the chap next door to do the job unless he is a dental surgeon. Surely then, on the same basis, one should select an instructor who has been *trained to teach*, in other words a qualified person.

The Road Traffic Act, 1962, introduces for the first time a Register of Approved Driving Instructors. To qualify, an Instructor must undertake a written and practical examination which is conducted by the Ministry of Transport. If successful the Instructor becomes a Ministry Approved Driving Instructor.

Free tuition by a relative or friend may be cheaper, but, with ever-rising insurance rates, father or the family friend may not be able to take the risk of a young learner at the wheel of his car. He may need his car for business and be unable to risk the repercussions of even a minor incident, which will lose him both his no-claim bonus and the use of his car whilst repairs are effected. Furthermore, while the incident may have damaged the car itself, far more important is the fact that it may have left a permanent dent in the confidence of the young learner involved.

Only the school of driving backed by long experience and capital resources can provide the necessary facilities, of which dual control is but one, that play such an important part when the learner is just beginning to feel his way. Equally, the relationship between father and son, however close, cannot match the professional basis on which instructor and learner meet. Only a professional can impart the necessary significance to his instructions that will ram home the lesson that motoring is a serious business and that the pleasure in it comes from the ability to drive well.

The success of this "master and pupil" principle is proved by the experience of *The British School of Motoring* who, some years ago, introduced a scheme in which driving lessons formed part of the general curriculum at schools, as an optional extra. At one girls' school a class of one hundred 17-year-old pupils were trained. All but six succeeded in passing the test at their first attempt, an instance which further underlines the advantage of learning young. Most important is the fact that these girls have received a sound foundation on which to base their future driving career. Prevention is better than cure which, in the motoring sense, means that education is better than legislation, which can only impose penalties on ignorance.

As we have said, there is little pleasure, and no pride to be derived from any activity unless one has the confidence born of knowledge. As far as driving is concerned there are two initial steps towards this before the learner can begin to acquire the third essential, which is experience.

One of these is a knowledge of the rules of the road. It is surprising how many learners approach the problem without first studying the Highway Code. Throughout the pages of this book we shall be quoting from it, but all drivers, whether learners or not, are required to know its contents* before taking out a licence. Its importance is emphasized by the following:

> "An applicant who, for the purpose of obtaining a licence knowingly makes any false statement, is liable to a fine not exceeding £100, or to imprisonment for a term not exceeding 4 months, or to both such imprisonment and fine."

* The Highway Code may be purchased direct from *Her Majesty's Stationery Office* at 49 High Holborn, London W.C.1; 13A Castle Street, Edinburgh EH2 3AR; Brazennose Street, Manchester M60 8AS; 258 Broad Street, Birmingham B1 2HE; 109 St. Mary Street, Cardiff CS1 1JW; 50 Fairfax Street, Bristol BS1 3DE; 80 Chichester Street, Belfast BT1 4JY; or through any bookseller.

2

---◆•••◆---

In the Driving Seat

Let us suppose you are now sitting at the wheel of a stationary car. The very first thing to do is to ensure that you are comfortably seated. Be warned by the classic statement of the anonymous musician in *The Lost Chord*:

> "*Seated one day at the organ*
> *I was weary and ill at ease.*"

If you *are* ill at ease you will not only become weary but you will be a danger to yourself and others on the road because you will not be in full control.

In all cars the driver's seat is adjustable to fairly close limits both backward and forward, and on a growing number of models, the seat-back upward and downward as well. Nevertheless present day seat design is a compromise, in that it tends to place considerations of cost and styling before the anatomical oddities of the human frame. Experiment will however soon find the most comfortable position, which will also be the most natural one. From it you should be able to depress the clutch pedal and the brake pedal without any forward movement of the body; in other words your shoulders should still rest against the back of the seat. It is important also that at all times the hollow of the back be adequately supported. For added confirmation that this position is the right one you should see that when the pedals are fully depressed your legs will still be bent. The reason for this is that if your legs are at full stretch you will find that quite unconsciously you will be gripping hard on the steering wheel to give you added thrust, which obviously must lessen your control over steering.

Holding the Steering Wheel

The steering wheel should never be gripped hard, nor
hung on to. It should be held firmly, but quite lightly. Furthermore it should be held in such a way as to combine the driver's
comfort with his efficiency. If one likens the steering wheel
to a clock-face the recommended position is between "ten
to two" and "quarter to three". This enables you to effect
any emergency movement of the wheel, and leaves arms and
elbows freedom of movement. This book does not set out to
cover high speed or any other advanced driving techniques
(see *High-Performance Driving for You* by Tom Wisdom—
published by Hamlyn) but nowhere is the example of a comfortable, relaxed driving position to enable full concentration
at the wheel better exemplified than in almost any photograph
of Graham Hill or Stirling Moss at speed.

The Highway Code also underlines this question of seating
for it lays down that "when driving you must be in such a
position that you can exercise proper control over your
vehicle and retain a full view of the traffic ahead".

The Dashboard

Let us now take a further look at things from the driving
seat. In front of you on the dashboard, or facia, is an array of
dials, knobs, press buttons and switches. The layout of these
will vary from car to car but their functions, of course, do not.
The more expensive the car the more detailed is the instru-
mentation, but every car is required by law to carry a speedometer to inform the driver of his speed; a total mileage
recorder is incorporated and sometimes, a trip recorder which
can be set to zero before the start of a journey. Another
essential visual aid is a petrol gauge calibrated in gallons or
marked off to denote the contents of the tank from "empty"

to "full".

It is well to remember that, although reasonably accurate, the petrol gauge is purely a guide to the contents of the tank, and an implicit belief in its accuracy can turn a motorist into a pedestrian at the most inconvenient times and places.

Dials are visual aids to driving but need to be looked at only from time to time. Not so the various control switches: these have to be operated by hand; the driver must know instinctively their positions and be able to find them without taking his eyes from the road just as the pianist will find the right notes upon the keyboard whilst his eyes remain on the music. Let us take a look at each of the important switches.

The Switches

(1) IGNITION SWITCH

The engine cannot start if the ignition switch is not turned on. It usually is operated by a Yale-type detachable key and when this is inserted in the lock and turned to the right the electric current stored in the battery flows through to the coil. When you have switched on you will notice that the petrol gauge, being electrically operated, now registers, and two small coloured lights, one red and one green or amber, have come on.

These two lights are warnings: the red informs you that the electrical current is being used. It should go out when the engine is started because the dynamo then begins to generate current to replace that used when the engine is running. If it remains on, or comes on at any time other than when the ignition is switched on prior to starting, it is a warning that your battery is discharging and requires attention. In some cars an ammeter gauge is fitted which registers the rate of charge or discharge.

Just as the red warning light has largely replaced the ammeter gauge, so has the green or amber light replaced the oil pressure gauge in the average family car. It operates on the same principle and lights up only as a warning that the flow of lubricating oil to the engine has stopped. It, too, should go out when the engine is started and the oil begins to circulate. If it does not do so, and you ignore the warning, the engine will suffer serious damage.

(2) STARTER SWITCH AND CHOKE CONTROL

The starter switch sometimes takes the form of a knob or button which is either pressed or pulled out. It is sometimes found on the floor to the left hand side of the driver or, more usually, on the facia. There is a growing and sensible tendency to incorporate this with the ignition switch and it is then operated by a further turn of the key to the right. If the engine responds to the starter the button or key should be released immediately. Do not hang on to it if the engine is reluctant to fire as this can exhaust the battery very quickly.

If the engine is to be started from cold or if it has lain idle for a long time, the starter must be operated in conjunction with the choke, which should be used only temporarily. The choke should not be used if the engine is warm. To ease the load on the battery the choke, by cutting off the air supply to the carburettor, gives a richer mixture of petrol gas to the cylinders and this makes starting easier—just as a neat brandy on certain occasions is more effective than one diluted by soda. However, both are temporary measures, and the choke should be pushed back to its original position once the engine is warm. Over-indulgence in either undiluted spirit is not to be recommended.

Automatic chokes, which come into operation with the starter switch and cut out when the engine reaches a certain temperature, are fitted to many cars and will, in due time, replace the manual choke entirely, so simplifying still further the actions of the man at the wheel.

(3) LIGHTING SWITCH AND DIPPER SWITCH

The Highway Code insists that "your vehicle has lights and reflectors which comply with the regulations," and the law requires that your car has two headlights, two white side lights, two red rear lights and two rear, red reflectors. It is also necessary that the rear number plate be illuminated. Needless to say, these lights must always be in working order.

Headlights are a necessity for night driving and the law now requires that where headlamps are fitted, and all cars have them, they must be used during *the hours of darkness* in any unlit area, i.e. where the street lamps are more than 200 yards apart. When they are on you will notice—on modern cars—that a pin point red light, marked "High Beam", appears on the speedometer (not to be confused with that other red warning light denoting battery discharge) and this reminds you that your headlights are at "full beam" position and may endanger drivers of oncoming vehicles by dazzling them. This too, can result in an offence against the law as it is laid down that "your headlights comply in particular with the anti-dazzle requirements". To this end a dipper switch, usually foot operated and placed on the floorboards to the left of the other foot controls, enables you to dip the beam and so reduce the danger. When this switch is pressed to dip headlight beam the red light will go out.

(4) WINDSCREEN WIPER SWITCH AND SCREEN WASHER

A clear field of vision through the windscreen is an obvious essential at all times, but particularly in rain or snow. It is also required by law, which insists that "your windscreen is clean and the windscreen wipers in working order". The wipers are controlled by a switch which, as with all the others, you should be able to reach and turn on without taking your eyes off the road. Another invaluable aid to good vision is the screen washer; on pressure of this a button pumps a jet of water on to the outside of the screen to aid the wipers in liquefying the fine layer of mud resulting from the spray thrown up by the wheels of other cars.

(5) TURN INDICATOR SWITCH

The turn indicators, or trafficators, as they are usually called, are used to give warning of your intention to other road users. In the main the original "semaphore" type of signal mounted high up on the body of the car, has now given way to the flashing light mounted low down on either side and fore and aft of the car. These indicators are operated by a lever mounted on the steering wheel column and usually are self-cancelling. This means they switch themselves off when the steering wheel is straightened after a turn. Their fitment is not yet a legal necessity, but if they are fitted they do have to conform to standards laid down by law. They *do not* take the place of all hand signals, which will be dealt with in detail elsewhere.

(6) ADDITIONAL LIGHTS AND SWITCHES

Many cars are fitted with "fog" or "pass" lights and the appropriate switches will be found on the dashboard. They are usually denoted by the letter "F" stamped on the switch itself and they are operated by a gentle pull. One fog lamp cannot be used on its own, but only in conjunction with the vehicle's headlamps. Headlamps may be extinguished provided two *permitted* auxiliary lamps are in operation.

In the majority of cases there is a panel-light switch fitted to the dashboard which, if operated when the side and tail lights are on, will illuminate the essential instruments, i.e. speedometer, oil-pressure gauge, water temperature and fuel gauge. This switch, by clockwise or anti-clockwise movement, will brighten or dim the light.

The car's interior light is hand operated; usually there is a switch on the light itself or it is fitted on the body-strip between the two offside doors. (Facing ahead in a car, the offside is on the driver's right, the nearside is on his left—the side of the car next to the kerb.) The interior light operates automatically when the car doors are open or at least it does if you own a fairly modern vehicle.

On the more expensive cars you will often find extras such as flashers for headlights, map-reading lights and individual reading lights.

If in doubt consult the instruction manual which should be supplied with the car.

(7) THE HORN

Usually the horn is in the form of a push button mounted in the centre of the steering wheel, although some cars are fitted with a horn ring, or semi-circular ring on the steering wheel which enables the driver to give audible warning of his approach without taking his hands from the wheel. It is an offence if your horn is not working, but the learner should also remember that it is also an offence to sound the horn in a built-up area between 11.30 p.m. and 7.00 a.m. or when the vehicle is stationary.

(8) THE BONNET LOCK

Only one other essential switch remains to be explained, and that is the simple bonnet lock which, when turned or pressed, releases a catch to enable the bonnet to be lifted for inspection of the engine or for the purpose of adding water to the radiator and battery and oil to the sump.

So much, then, for the controls which confront you as you sit at the wheel for the first time. We have explained the operation of the essential ones, but have purposely omitted reference to such optional equipment as for instance, the revolution counter, or tachometer (which indicates engine speed in revolutions per minute), switches to operate heater, ventilator, radio, fuel-tank change-over, and other refinements which may be found on more expensive cars, or may be added to a family car as extras by the driver himself.

The position of all control switches must be learned before the pupil sets out on his first drive. A split-second saved in finding and using a control may make all the difference in an emergency. In our experience the best method is that employed by the R.A.F.: reading left to right layer by layer from the top row, but this is largely a matter for the learner himself. Remember, too, that the instruments in front of you are for your information. When you are driving take a cursory glance from time to time to check that all is well. See that you have enough fuel in your tank; see that the red and green or amber warning lights are not showing and that your speed is restricted to the legal limit when one applies.

3

The Major Controls

In the preceding chapter we discussed the object and operations of the various controls grouped on the facia, or around the steering wheel and column. Although they all play their own individual and corporate part let us call them the minor controls to differentiate these from the major controls of steering wheel, gear lever, clutch and brake pedals and accelerator, or "gas" pedal as we shall henceforth call it. In other words those that require a co-ordination of movement by the driver's hands and feet rather than those that require only to be pushed, pulled or turned to operate.

The ability to handle these controls with ease, accuracy, dexterity and sympathy is the key to good driving.

The Steering Wheel

We touched earlier and briefly upon the steering wheel and how to hold it in relation to a comfortable driving position, but there is much more to it than that. It is a primary lesson of car control that the vehicle be always in the right place on the road, and it is the job of the driver to see that it is so by safe and accurate steering.

Safety and accuracy are best obtained by holding the wheel about the "ten to two" position at all times to ensure freedom for necessary arm movements and to effect any rapid movement of the wheel that may be required in emergency. However, when turning to the right or left this freedom would be lost if your hands remained at "ten to two" because you would

finish the manoeuvre with hands and arms crossed; a position
in which your control of the car would be difficult in the
extreme. In addition, control would be further endangered by
your having to relinquish hold upon the wheel in order to
regain the correct position.

This is a safe, restful position.

So, to make a turn this is what you must do. The hand on
the side of the wheel corresponding to the turn to be made
(i.e. the right hand for a right turn, the left for a left) is moved
to a position where the wheel can be pulled over and down in
the direction of the turn. This position is above (but not over)
the other hand which holds position but allows the wheel rim
to slide through it. In this way, when your turn is completed,
both hands are still at "ten to two".

Try this for yourself. You wish to turn right; so you remove
your right hand from the wheel and place it above your left
hand. With your right hand you pull the wheel to the right
whilst allowing the wheel rim to slide through your left hand

without relinquishing hold. When your manoeuvre is completed you will find both hands are in the accustomed and recommended position of "ten to two". To turn left it is the left hand which is moved upward on the steering wheel and over to the right. The right hand allows the wheel rim to slide through its grasp whilst the left pulls the wheel over in the designed direction of the hand.

This exercise should be practised by the learner until it becomes both natural and automatic, but only in dummy motions, because the wheels of a stationary car should *not* be turned lest damage by strain be caused to the steering mechanism. In any case the physical strain of moving the wheel of a stationary car would be too great.

Having negotiated your turn, the road wheels must be straightened; the steering wheel should be fed back by similar movements, but in reverse. On some cars self-centring action will bring the wheel back to its normal position, in which case the driver allows the wheel rim to slide through his grasp until the car reverts to a straight course. This again underlines the necessity for a firm but relaxed grip upon the steering wheel.

A relaxed grip is not always easy for the novice driver to acquire because, tense and apprehensive, he tends to grasp the steering wheel too tightly. This is physically tiring and makes for the sort of jerky and uneven movements of the wheel which can, in certain conditions, induce a skid. The grip should be firm, but light. Always be ready to tighten your hold for added control when cornering or braking. As with all aspects of better, safer motoring, correct steering comes from experience, but do not let familiarity breed contempt. Drive always with your hands on the wheel about the "ten to two" position. Remember that if you have suddenly to change direction to avoid a dangerous situation you must have control of the car through your steering wheel. You will not be able to exercise that control if your right elbow is resting on the window ledge and your fingers are curled round the spokes of the wheel.

To steer the car going backwards, that is, in reverse, calls for similar basic movements. The wheel is turned right if you wish to reverse in that direction, and left if you wish to reverse left. This manoeuvre will be dealt with fully in a later chapter.

One further point; to steer correctly it is obviously necessary to see clearly where you are going. The best view is straight ahead at eye level, for there you have an 180-degree width of vision. The farther ahead you can focus your gaze the straighter and more quickly can you drive. But if your focus is limited by a gradient or a twist in the road your speed must be correspondingly reduced, as it would be if your view ahead was obstructed by another car. Other aids to good vision, and thus to good driving, are a comfortable seating position and a clean windscreen.

The handbrake will be dealt with in the next section, in association with the brake pedal.

Foot Controls

At your feet will be found three other major controls consisting of, from left to right, clutch pedal, brake pedal and accelerator, which we call the gas pedal. It has been found from long experience in teaching people to drive that to say "more gas", or "less gas" is less confusing to the novice than to say "accelerator down" or "accelerator up".

These three pedals have considerable influence on driving ease and efficiency. It is most important to get to know the "feel" of them. Obviously, their tension and, to some degree their type, varies with the make of the car, but the whole success of the driver is dependent upon the smoothness with which they are operated and manipulated in conjunction with each other.

Let us take the gas pedal first.

Gas Pedal

This controls the acceleration and deceleration of the car. Acceleration is the increase in road speed brought about by the pressure exerted by the driver with the right foot on the gas pedal. More gas means more speed. Less gas means less speed.

To illustrate this we will start the car. First, the ignition is switched on; then we check that the gear lever is in neutral and the choke control is pulled out (if required). The ignition key is turned and the engine starts. It is regulated to "tick over" at slow speed without any assistance from your right foot. When the engine is warm the choke control is pushed back to the closed position. If pressure is applied to the gas pedal the flow of petrol gas to the carburettor is increased and a correspondingly greater volume of the combustible mixture of gas and air is admitted to the cylinders. This mixture produces an increase in engine revolutions per minute which, when transmitted to the driving wheels turns them quicker and thus the car accelerates. When this pressure is released, or lifted (less gas) the revolutions fall, and speed is reduced.

The gas pedal can be likened to the wick of an oil lamp. Turn it up and you get more light; turn it down and the flame goes dim. Indeed it is a simile much used by motor cyclists who talk of "I turned the wick up" as a more graphic and descriptive way of saying, "I accelerated". Unlike the wick, however, the gas pedal is foot operated and it is also spring loaded to return to the closed position when not under pressure. It is the "feel" of this spring loading that must be acquired to attain a smooth even increase and decrease in road speed. Smooth progression will come from experience, but experience teaches slowly at the cost of mistakes. However, these can be reduced by two precautions: always wear light shoes, because it is difficult to get an accurate "feel" if the soles of your footwear are thick, and, second, be sure that your right foot is correctly placed to work the gas pedal; the heel should rest on the floorboard so that it may be used as a pivot to operate the pedal by the toe of the shoe. It must be remembered that when the car is in motion the gas pedal will be in almost constant use, and a comfortable position for the right foot is essential.

Clutch Pedal

The driving force of the motor car, in other words the power that is provided to enable it to travel forwards or backwards, comes, naturally, from the engine. So far we have dealt with how to steer the vehicle on its course, and how to make it go faster or slower by pressure upon the gas pedal. To illustrate this we started the engine, but the car remained stationary. If the running engine is to move the car it is necessary to connect it to the driving wheels which, dependent upon the make of car, may be the front wheels (as, for instance, with the Citroen and the B.M.C. range of mini-cars), or, more generally, the back wheels. Drive on all four wheels is found on certain heavy-duty vehicles for special purposes, but it does not concern us here.

This connexion is brought about by the clutch. This consists of two discs or plates, one of them stationary, the other revolving; the latter being attached to the engine. To bring about the necessary contact between engine and driving wheels the rotating disc must come together with the stationary disc which is attached through the gearbox to the driving wheels. Contact is obtained by the clutch pedal, which is to be found on the left of the brake pedal and gas pedal. It is operated by the left foot. When, in Chapter Two, we discussed the importance of a good driving position we said that it should be possible to depress the clutch pedal to the limit of its travel without any forward movement of the body, and also that when the clutch pedal was fully depressed your left leg should still be bent. The reason for this is the need for the two discs of the clutch to be connected easily and smoothly. A correct driving position will have a bearing upon this operation. If the clutch pedal is operated smoothly the drive will be taken up smoothly; if however the pedal is operated harshly the engine will stop and the car will "stall". The moving disc and the stationary disc must be brought together gradually so that the moving one will "clutch" the stationary one and the two discs will then turn as one.

If the car gearbox is in neutral, depression and release of the clutch pedal alone will not get the vehicle to move; this happens only if a gear has been engaged, and will be explained in detail under the appropriate heading.

Before doing so let us examine more closely the operation of the clutch pedal. The learner will find that some physical effort is required to depress the clutch, but much less to release it. This is because the two discs are spring loaded to bring them together, and to separate them is obviously harder than to rejoin them. You push against them to depress the clutch (and so separate the discs) but the springs are working "on your side" when you allow the clutch pedal to come up (and so join the discs). Effective clutch operation, therefore, lies in the correct relaxation of the clutch pedal. Release it too quickly and the car will leap forward and, quite likely, the engine will stall. Release it too slowly and you may do damage by allowing the clutch plates to rub on one another so generating heat by friction and "burning out" the clutch by destroying the material on the faces of its discs.

We have said before and shall repeat that in the smooth operation of the controls lies the art of good driving. A racing driver is said to control his car by the seat of his pants, and in that there is an element of truth. Delicacy of touch on gas pedal and clutch pedal can be acquired by continual practice, providing all faults have been eradicated in the tuition period.

There are two important faults to be avoided. They can be

avoided if the learner remembers that the clutch is normally used only when either engaging or disengaging a gear. So when the gear change has been made the left foot must not be kept on the clutch pedal. It must never be held half in and half out, for this will cause the revolving disc to slide over the stationary one without the drive being taken up. This in turn will cause clutch slip and generate friction which will render the clutch inoperative by destroying the facings of the clutch plates.

The second common fault is "riding the clutch". All clutches are so adjusted that there is a small amount of play in the pedal before it does its job of separating the discs. This free movement is a form of insurance in that it allows for slight wear upon the surface of the discs, but if the learner continually rests his foot upon the clutch pedal this play will be eliminated by unnecessary wear. There is a tendency to do this owing to the position of the pedal, but it is a habit that must be avoided at all costs.

The clutch pedal is placed on the left-hand side of the three controls because it is operated in conjunction with the gas pedal and both are used in conjunction with each other in the act of gear changing. Thus the left foot operates the clutch pedal whilst the right foot operates the gas pedal.

Brake Pedal and Lever

The right foot also operates the brake pedal which is placed between the clutch and gas pedals. The duty of the brakes, of course, is to bring the car to stop whenever required. There are two braking controls, the footbrake and the handbrake.

A car is required by law to have an independent means of braking on the rear wheels, and to meet this requirement a handbrake is fitted. It is operated either by an umbrella-type handle on, or just below the facia, or by a lever usually to be found mounted centrally in the car to the left of the driver's seat. Being an "independent means of braking" it is cable operated and so is not dependent upon the hydraulic system of braking which is operated by the footbrake. It is purely an emergency brake, and should be treated as such; its chief use is to prevent a car moving when parked.

The handbrake works upon a ratchet and pawl; a locking device operates as a safety measure when the brake is on. This lock is usually in the form of a button or a trigger at the end of the lever or, in the case of the umbrella type, it is locked on by a twist or a turn of the handle. To release the handbrake the trigger must be depressed to disengage the lock.

Of all the pedals the brake pedal is perhaps the simplest, the one most easily understood by the novice. By its application the speed of the car is reduced. It operates hydraulically on all four wheels, usually with the assistance of a servo unit which reduces the pressure required to apply the brakes without in any way impairing their efficiency.

Although it does not perhaps call for quite the same delicacy of touch required by the clutch and gas pedals, the footbrake must be operated with intelligence and skill. Reducing speed by the application of the brakes can be hazardous because of its effect upon the car. There are, therefore, a number of points regarding its use to be borne in mind.

A degree of braking can be effected by taking the right foot off the gas pedal. But often this is not enough. The footbrake augments the reduction in speed by a degree dependent upon pedal pressure and time; in other words, the harder you push, the quicker you stop.

The quickness with which a vehicle stops is dependent upon two things; the driver's reaction to the need to brake and the speed at which the car is moving. There is a recognized set of figures which explains it in diagrammatic form, far better than words; this should be carefully studied on page 107.

Remember also that you should brake only when travelling in a straight line. Try not to brake when turning a corner and never use your brakes when skidding. Always brake smoothly whether applying or releasing the pedal; this is especially important when the road surface is slippery. Never apply your brakes unnecessarily: try to gauge your speed accordingly because a car is more stable under acceleration than when it is braking.

4

The Gears

We have explained the function and operation of all the controls, major and minor, with the important exception of the gears and the lever with which they are selected. In the previous chapter we explained that the two clutch discs, or plates, when brought together connected the engine to the driving wheels through the medium of the gearbox.

So let us now take a closer look at the gearbox. The majority of modern cars are equipped with four forward gears and a reverse, but there are still some to be found with three forward gears. The gears are all of a different ratio, designed to do a different job, but chosen with the overall view of providing the best performance possible from the engine under widely varying situations.

How They Work

To explain the use of gearing let us draw a simple analogy. You will remember from your school days the lesson that to overcome inertia requires more power than is needed to keep anything on the move once it is moving. Let us suppose you are standing still and you start to walk. This requires some initial effort and until you get into your stride the steps you will take will be short. In effect, you are in low, or bottom gear; your legs are moving fast, but you are going slowly. To maintain these short steps is tiring and wasteful of energy, and so your stride lengthens into an easier, faster progression until you reach the rate you require. Thus you have moved up through your gears until you are in high, or top gear, which is the most economical as it uses up no more energy than your quick, short steps, and yet enables you to cover the ground more quickly.

Obviously you will adjust your stride to changing conditions; on a hill your long strides will shorten again because that way it is easier for you to climb. Your shorter steps give you greater power but less speed. The steeper the hill, the shorter your steps and thus you choose for yourself the correct gear ratio to climb the hill with the greatest ease. So, too in traffic: whilst you are walking in the open country your step will be a long, easy top-gear one. But when you are walking in a busy town, with the pavement crowded by other people all walking in different directions at different speeds, your stride will shorten and your speed will fall, so making it easier for you to negotiate the hazards.

Only in the case of reverse gear does our analogy fail to work, because if you wish to retrace your steps you will turn around to do so, despite the conflicting evidence given by those famous Goons in their song "I'm Walking Backwards For Christmas".

The reason for gears and gearing is best summed up by saying that they permit the engine to work hard when hard work is required of it, but they allow the engine to take it easy when the going is easy.

The spacing of the gear ratios varies from car to car and is dependent upon a number of factors, amongst them the size of engine and the power it develops, the back-axle ratio and the size of tyres. This need not concern the learner; all he should remember is that in bottom gear the engine speed is high and the road speed is low whereas in top gear the engine speed is proportionately low to the high road speed.

With the engine working less hard in top gear it is obvious that engine wear will be much reduced and better fuel consumption figures will be obtained; but to get the best from your car an intelligent use of the gearbox is essential.

Each gear has its maximum speed. That is to say, a steady unchanging pressure on the gas pedal will result in a gradual increase of road speed as each gear is selected one after another until top is engaged. It is important to grasp the fact that the lower the gear the more quickly will the car gain speed up to the maximum obtainable in that gear. As a case in point let us say that you are travelling at 25 m.p.h. and wish to pass the car in front of you which is doing the same speed. Provided that the way is clear you will give the engine more gas and pull out to pass. It will, however, take a little time for the engine to respond to your demands because it is in top gear. If you change down to a lower gear and give more gas the engine will respond that much more quickly and your manoeuvre will be completed in far less time, which makes for greater safety because the longer you take to pass another car the longer you are in the path of oncoming traffic.

Because he is unaccustomed to the operation of gear changing a common fault with the learner driver is a tendency to hang on to top gear once it has been attained. Though it is natural for the learner to hesitate to change gear, failure to do so can be extremely bad for the engine, which should never be allowed to "labour" in top gear up hills, for instance. Neither should the car be allowed to run in top gear at too low a road speed since this will cause it to move along in a series of jerks which is bad for the transmission and may result in the engine stalling. Just as, when walking, you anticipate the need to shorten your stride when there are other pedestrians ahead of you, so should you always anticipate the need for a lower gear when such obstacles as other traffic, or corners, loom up before you. You will have more control over your car in a lower gear when lower speeds are called for.

The Gear Lever

Our next step is to take a look at the lever with which the gears are changed in co-ordination with the clutch and gas pedal. This lever is connected to the gearbox and is placed conveniently near the steering wheel. Today there are two main types: that mounted immediately beneath, and usually, to the left of the steering wheel, and the other consisting of a lever mounted centrally on the floor at the side of the driving seat. It is usual to find marked on the knob of this lever, or in some appropriate place, the position into which it must be moved to obtain the requisite gear. When the lever is in neutral it can be freely moved from side to side. Some sort of safety device is usually incorporated to prevent the accidental selection of reverse gear. The novice must learn to get into reverse gear as well as the position of all the forward gears before any attempt is made to drive the car.

Clutch, Gear Lever and Gas Pedal

Let us try a dummy run. We will imagine that our car has a floor-mounted gear change to the left of the driver, and that the box contains five gears, four forward and one reverse. There are, thus, six positions for the lever, for we must not forget neutral. Our first job before starting will always be to check that the lever is in neutral, that is to say, that the car is out of gear. To engage first gear our left foot depresses the clutch pedal and our left hand moves the gear lever to the appropriate position. The clutch is then released gently at the same time as our right foot applies more pressure to the gas pedal so that the engine power is connected to the driving wheels as smoothly as possible.

To move from first to second gear the clutch is depressed again and the gear lever pulled back into neutral, pausing for a moment whilst the right foot eases pressure on the gas pedal, then the lever is moved into second gear whilst the clutch is released and at the same time the engine is given more gas to increase speed.

From second to third is a little more difficult to begin with as it involves a longer and diagonal travel to its new position, but the foot movements are the same; the clutch is depressed as the lever is moved through neutral to third, the gas pedal is eased and then as the clutch is released the gas pedal is given more pressure. From third to top gear will be the same movement as from first to second.

In every gear change, whether up or down, the lever must pass through neutral, and in every *upward* change the gas pedal pressure will be lifted momentarily as the "no man's land" of neutral is negotiated, and then increased again as the drive takes up its new gear. It has to be remembered that the higher the gear the more slowly the engine turns.

Just as the gas pedal pressure is eased while the gear lever is in neutral en route from one gear to another when changing up, so the pressure is increased at the same point when changing down. In both instances this is to adjust the engine speed to enable a smooth and silent change to be effected. So remember; changing up, less gas; changing down, more gas.

Do not be disheartened if this takes a little time to master for, after all, one of the biggest problems of the learner driver is the co-ordination of clutch pedal, gas pedal and gear lever. Whilst his left foot is pressing down on one pedal his right must be raised off another, and whilst his left hand moves the gear lever in any one of the several directions his right must remain steady on the steering wheel and all these inter-related movements must be automatic whilst his eyes and all his attention is held on the road ahead.

A really good gear change can bring a thrill of pleasure but at least a bad one is no longer as noticeable as it was before the introduction of synchromesh.

Double-declutching

This mechanism is designed to make gear changing, if not foolproof, certainly easier and quieter. Its application to almost every modern car has made the business of double-declutching unnecessary. As a refinement to the art of gear changing double-declutching is no longer essential but it is the most successful method for the learner.

We have already described in detail the various actions involved in changing gear. Each change involved, amongst other movements, the depression and release of the clutch pedal once, and once only. Double-declutching means what it says: the clutch is depressed and released twice for each change. It is depressed once to enable the gear lever to be moved into neutral, released, then depressed again to engage the next gear and, once the lever is in the new position, the clutch is of course released again. This double movement of the left foot also makes it easier for the right foot, the gas pedal foot, to remember its job; for whenever the left foot is *down* on the clutch the right foot will be *up* off the gas pedal: and whenever the left foot is *up*, the right will be down. To clarify this further we set out below the sequence of operations for a gear change. Let us call it a symphony divided into four movements. Played correctly the sweet music of a perfect gear change will result:

1st movement: Clutch pedal depressed (down) gas pedal raised (up) lever into neutral.

2nd movement: Clutch pedal released (up) gas pedal (down)

3rd movement: Clutch pedal depressed (down) gas pedal raised (up) lever into gear.

4th movement: Clutch pedal released (up) gas pedal (down).

One other important aspect of the gearbox is its use in

engine braking. Give your car more gas and it will go faster, lift your foot off and the speed will drop. However the degree of slowing down depends upon the gear you are in and the lower the gear the quicker will the car slow down. Thus normal braking can be greatly assisted by a change down and of course with the right foot off the gas pedal. Going down a steep hill for instance, it is unwise to stay in top gear and rely upon normal braking to retard your progress. It is much safer, and much better for your car, to change down to a gear appropriate to the gradient (the steeper the hill the lower the gear) and let your engine augment the brake pressure. This holds good at all times when traffic is congested and roundabouts, corners and other hazards have to be negotiated. It also means that you are in the appropriate gear to accelerate when the time is right and it is perhaps unnecessary to remind you once again that you have much more control over your car in a lower gear when lower speeds are necessary.

Never be afraid to use your gearbox. Learn to use it well, because its proper use marks the good driver immediately, not only in the precise, co-ordinated manipulations of the controls concerned, but in his intuitive choice of the correct gear for every road speed and condition.

Constant practice will help you to attain this desired end, and experience will, in time, perfect it. However, for those who feel they will never master its complexities, there is an alternative method of two-pedal control, or automatic transmission, which we will deal with in the next chapter.

5

Two-Pedal Control

In the United States some 80% of cars are fitted with automatic transmission, or two-pedal control, as normal equipment and have been for twenty years. This is largely due to the traffic density in that country giving impetus to the development of automatic transmission which eliminates the physical effort involved in continual gear changing in such conditions. With the ever-increasing traffic in this country automatic transmission may be expected to make similar strides over here. Indeed, many experts consider that it is only a matter of time before the clutch pedal is rendered obsolete.

For that, briefly, is what automatic transmission does. It does away with the clutch pedal leaving you only with the brake pedal to stop with and the gas pedal to "go" with. The obvious simplification of two pedals and two feet need hardly be emphasized.

Over here in the post-war years a number of adaptations of American designs have been available on large cars, as well as some forms of semi-automatic transmission and, in one case, a belt-driven type on a small European car. It is only recently, however, that a fully automatic transmission has been made suitable for the medium-sized (and priced) family car, and it is the workings of this particular car we outline here in general terms.

One disadvantage of automatic transmission is that it is as difficult to explain its workings as it is easy to operate. The learner need not, therefore, be unduly concerned if he fails to grasp the technicalities. In the main the unit consists of two components. One is an hydraulic torque converter which replaces the conventional flywheel and clutch and provides a fluid connexion between the engine and the gearbox. The other is an hydraulically-operated automatic gearbox which provides three forward speeds and one reverse.

In addition to the disappearance of the clutch pedal the gear lever is also dispensed with. In its place, but mounted on the steering column, is a hand control lever and a selector marked with initials; let us first explain these.

D for Drive. In this position, which is used for all normal driving conditions, the transmission starts in first gear and automatically changes up into second and then top gear depending upon road speed and gas pedal pressure. With decreasing speed the gears will change down from top to second and to first at the appropriate times. A change down can be effected at the driver's will by "kickdown", that is by depressing the gas pedal with sufficient force to overcome the spring loaded plunger (or detent, as it is called) which is at the apparent limit of travel of the gas pedal.

N for Neutral. Needs no explanation. Only in this position or in *Park* can the engine be started.

P for Park. Identical to neutral except that in *Park* the gearbox is locked and thus the car is completely immobilized.

R for Reverse. Also speaks for itself.

L for Lock-up. With the selection of *Lock-up* the driver is enabled to override the automatic sequence. If it is selected from getaway the car will start in first gear and remain in it as long as the lever stays in "L" irrespective of road speed or pressure on the gas pedal. It provides maximum engine braking also. When selected at speeds up to 20 m.p.h. an immediate change down to first takes place and the transmission remains locked there with full engine braking. If *Lock-up* is selected at speeds over 20 m.p.h. second gear is engaged from top and once again it will remain there and provide engine braking. At speeds below 10 m.p.h. the transmission will

engage first gear from second and remain there until the lever
is moved. Furthermore up to 20 m.p.h. first gear can also be
obtained by use of the "kickdown".

Thus it will be seen that, if required, a high degree of
individual choice of gears to override the automatic selection
is available to give the driver the benefits of both worlds,
manual and automatic.

Automatic Gear Change in Action

Driving procedure is as follows. First the driver will make
sure that the selector is in the *Neutral* or *Park* position. A
safety device does, in fact, prevent the engine from being
started in any of the other positions. With the engine running,
Drive is selected, the handbrake released, and a gentle pressure
on the gas pedal will set the car in motion. It is a feature of
automatic transmission that a start from rest is always smooth
regardless of the gas pedal pressure.

From this point on, the car will automatically change upward through the gears at points which are dependent upon
gas pedal pressure. For instance, light pressure will bring the
upward changes quite quickly at low speeds. If the gas pedal is
pressed down to the limit of the detent these changes will occur
at higher speeds with correspondingly longer intervals between
them, and if the pedal is pressed through the detent the changes
take place at the maximum road speeds for each gear. These,
being present, prevent the engine from being overstressed, but
are designed to give peak performance in each ratio.

To allow the automatic changes down to occur the gas
pedal pressure is lightened and the same sequence of changes
occur. However, there are times when a lower gear is required
without delay and this is obtained by the "kickdown", that is,
by pressing the gas pedal hard enough to overcome the detent.
Thus second, or first gear is immediately available for overtaking, climbing hills or in any emergency. Thus, despite the

automatic operation, the driver retains a quite considerable degree of control purely by the intelligent manipulation of his gas pedal.

Even more individual control can be exercised by the selection of *Lock-up* which has already been described.

There are a number of other points peculiar to automatic transmission which must be remembered, notably that the right foot must always be taken off the gas pedal and pressure applied to the brake pedal before selecting *Reverse* or either of the two forward positions *Drive* and *Lock-up*. The reason for this is that there is a certain amount of "creep" because of the high idling, or tick-over speed of the engine. This "creep" can be most useful when manoeuvring into, and out of, confined spaces.

In addition *Park* or *Reverse* must not be selected whilst the car is moving, neither should *Lock-up* be selected at speeds over 55 m.p.h. except in an emergency.

Emergency starts, necessitated by a flat battery or other cause, can be made by tow, or push starting. To effect such a start the car should be allowed to reach a speed of about 25 m.p.h. with the selector in *Neutral*. The ignition should then be switched on and *Lock-up* selected.

The question as to whether the left foot should be used for braking leaving the right solely to operate the gas pedal is still a matter of individual choice particularly in this country where automatic transmission is not as widely used as it is in the United States. To drivers who regularly drive cars with and without automatic transmission there is a possible risk of confusion if they employ one technique one day and another the next. However, drivers, and particularly learner drivers, should at least try left-foot braking because reaction delay in any emergency can be reduced for there is no time lost whilst moving the right foot from the gas pedal to the brake pedal.

Because in Britain relatively few cars are as yet equipped with automatic transmission a learner will, unless he states a definite preference for it, be taught to drive on cars with the conventional form of drive. It is our experience, however, that it is best to learn on the manual type and later go over to the automatic. As the use of automatic transmission becomes more general, as it certainly will, bringing with it simpler, safer motoring on our traffic-congested roads, the methods of instruction will have to be amended.

6

———— ❖ ————

Getting Set to Go

After five chapters on theory the learner may be forgiven for a little impatience. He is naturally anxious to exchange the theory for the practice, the open text book for the open road. Nevertheless, what has gone before, if he has fully assimilated it all, is going to stand him in good stead. Thorough understanding of what one is going actually to practise in the driving seat means a clear idea of all that driving involves and that will help to make a better, safer driver for today's conditions.

Nothing in life is free. Freedom of movement and the pleasure that is obtainable from driving a car must be paid for by the full acceptance of the responsibility of driving it. If, in business, you are promoted to take control of a department you must also accept the responsibility along with the control. Throughout these pages we have made mention of the Highway Code, and before you slip into the driving seat on your first run on the highway let us just return to this for a moment. In it are contained the rules of the road which you must know and obey. Every road user is bound by them and you are no exception.

The main rule of the road in Britain is that you drive on the left-hand side of the road, and on that side you will stay except when pulling out to overtake, or turning right or in one-way streets. In abbreviated form the Highway Code lays down a code of behaviour for every situation in which a road-user may find himself or herself. Many things in the Code will not be fully understood and appreciated until the learner has some experience on the road, but the basic elementary rules to which he must conform from the very outset of his driving career must be learned. The application of the less obvious rules will be met in the course of his early drives with his instructor and their general use will become clearer as the various manoeuvres are associated with the appropriate paragraph in the Code.

Signs

As he drives along he will be confronted with various road signs. On the end-papers of this book he will see illustrations of some of these signs, the meaning of which, it is hoped, he has committed to memory. They should be studied and learned even though their meanings may not be immediately apparent, for they give valuable information and important commands to drivers.

The signs fall into three main categories, Regulatory, Warning and Informatory.

Regulatory signs are covered by an Act of Parliament and thus must be obeyed; failing to do so leaves you open to prosecution. Amongst these are such signs as "No Waiting", "No Entry", "Give Way", "Stop" and the speed limit signs of "30", "40", "50", "60" and "70" m.p.h. All signs of this sort are distinguishable by a red circle, or the sign itself is contained within a red border; a few have a blue circle.

The second type is the warning sign which carries a red triangle, and warns of such hazards ahead as schools and level crossings, bends, roundabouts and the like. It is not laid down by law that these signs be acted upon, but to ignore the warnings that they give is not the conduct of a good driver and failure to take precautions after being so warned could lead to an accident and even to prosecution.

Informatory signs are the third type and, as their name implies, are for information only. Varying from the large modern direction type as found on motorways to the simple signpost, they tell you what road you are on, how many miles distant is the next town or village, and much other useful information.

Signals

The next point with which the Highway Code deals and which now assumes considerable importance to the learner is the question of hand signals. By these means he communicates his intentions to others on the road. They are solely an indication of his intentions; they are not instructions or orders to others. Here again the basic information is in the Highway Code which lists the three hand signals. They are simple and straightforward and if given clearly, decisively and in good time avoid any possible misunderstanding.

The car of today is fitted with direction indicators in the form of flashing lights operated from a switch on the facia, or by lever on the steering column and these should be used at all times to indicate your intentions. Other mechanical signals under the driver's control are the brake lights which come up on the application of the brakes to warn the following car, and that "audible warning of approach", the horn. As previously mentioned in Chapter Two it is an offence to sound the horn when stationary and in a built-up area between the hours of 11.30 p.m. and 7.00 a.m., but when it is legal and necessary to use it, do so politely. The sudden blast immediately behind someone is not just rude but frightening as well and arouses antagonism. A gentle reminder that you are there and wish to pass is more than enough. As a learner you will often find yourself on the receiving end of many an impatient, arrogant blast from drivers you have unwittingly, and through inexperience, impeded, drivers who once wore L-plates just like you. Try to remember this when you are an experienced driver. That they have forgotten reflects no credit upon them.

Candidates in the driving test are not expected to give signals at *all* times regardless of circumstances. However, since it is most important that other road-users should know well in advance what change of speed or direction is intended, learner-drivers should be taught that signals (whether by indicator or by hand) are omitted only when no other road-user could benefit from them. This refers not only to following traffic but to road-users of any kind moving in any direction, including pedestrians.

Learner-drivers should give directional signals by hand *or* by indicator, not by a combination of both. The candidate who does not make use of hand signals during the first half of the test is normally asked to give signals by hand exclusively for a time, to enable the Examiner to assess his competence to give hand signals. It follows that where an Examiner has observed hand signals given satisfactorily he does not normally thereafter make any reference to signals during the drive.

The process of using a combination of "slow down" and "turning" signals prior to making a left or right turn occupies time which is better devoted to the directional signal. The directional signal is all-important and if this signal is given correctly and in good time there is no need for any other signal.

Before you get into the car with your instructor he will want to show you the vehicle. The two of you have not met and the instructor will make the introduction. He will show you round the car, and it is a habit worth cultivating always to walk round your car if it has been standing for any time. A "hit and run" driver may have scraped a wing, a tyre may need more air or someone may have brushed some broken glass into the gutter over which you will run when you start away. The instructor will open up the bonnet to show you the engine and the position of the various component parts, such as the carburettor, battery, distributor, fuse box, fan belt, the steering box, radiator and the like. As we have said, it is not essential that you know the workings of the internal combustion engine; for the moment learning to drive is enough and technical "know-how" can be acquired later.

Once in the driving seat, you can begin to put your newly-acquired knowledge to the test. Settle yourself comfortably and make any necessary adjustments to enable you to operate the foot controls without strain. Remember that your legs should still be bent when the clutch and brake pedals are fully depressed. Now switch on the ignition to check that your instruments are in order and that there is enough fuel in the tank. You have naturally made certain that both your own door and the passenger's are properly shut. You have also checked that the gear lever is in the neutral position and the handbrake on. For this first occasion, we will assume that your instructor has satisfied himself that the tyres have been inflated to the correct pressures, that there is the right amount of water in the radiator and that there is enough oil in the sump. We mention these three essential points here, however, because when you have become a fully-fledged motorist you will be responsible for checking air, oil and water yourself. Neglect of the fundamental items before driving the car could lead to inconvenience and to serious trouble and expense, not to mention danger.

Looking Backwards

Only one thing remains to be done before starting up and that is to adjust the driving mirror so that you have full available rearward vision. Up to now, we have purposely omitted any mention of the rear mirror in order to emphasize its importance at this stage when the learner is about to take to the road. In today's traffic, it is almost as essential to see the traffic pattern developing behind you as it is to see what is going on in front of you. The habit is not easy to cultivate, but the beginner must learn to look frequently into his rear mirror throughout the journey. Indeed, it is estimated that a good driver glances into his mirror every six or seven seconds.

These preparations all completed, the starter button is

pressed or the ignition key is given a further turn and while
the engine warms up you take another quick look at the dials.
The oil pressure is working, as you can tell because the green
or amber warning light goes off when you give the gas pedal a
quick dab. Similarly, you know that the battery is charging
because the red ignition light has also gone out. Engage first
gear, glance over shoulder and look in the mirror to make sure
all is clear behind and—the final instruction—use your indicator to show that you are about to move off. Do this whether
your glance in the rear view mirror has told you there is a
distant vehicle behind you or not. This may strike you as unnecessary, even slightly crazy. But there is method in our
madness. Of course, an experienced driver who had checked
that no traffic was coming up behind him would not make a
signal just for the sake of it. But you are not yet an experienced
driver and it is desirable that you should get into the habit
early of making your intentions clear to all other road users.

However, as you become more experienced you will only
signal when necessary but bear in mind that there may always
be a pedestrian or cyclist about who could benefit from a signal.

And now, at last, we are ready to move off. Such a long
awaited event, we are sure you agree, deserves a chapter to
itself.

"Mirror, Mirror on the screen,
What's behind I haven't seen. . . ."

7

On the Move

The engine is purring nicely and the road ahead beckons invitingly. Four basic and inter-related functions must be mastered before you can accept that invitation with enjoyment and in safety: starting; accelerating by use of the gears; steering; and stopping. Never forget that driving is a skill. Like all skills, improvement comes with experience. The old saw that "practice makes perfect" applies equally to driving, only with this proviso: that the more experienced a driver becomes, the more he realizes that he has *not* reached perfection. There is always room for improvement. So do not be discouraged if the attempts you are about to make to set the car in motion are not immediately satisfactory. You are already on the path to improvement.

Right. Now depress the clutch pedal to its fullest extent and move the gear lever into first gear position. Check your mirror and signal with your indicator if necessary. As you release the handbrake slowly let the clutch pedal come up, at the same time pressing gently on the gas pedal until you feel the gears engage and the car begins to move forward. Properly co-ordinated movement of the clutch and gas pedals will result in a smooth take-off. Too-sudden engagement of the clutch or too much pressure on the gas pedal results either in the engine stalling or in that jerky motion, somewhat reminiscent of a bucking bronco, which most new drivers experience at some time or another. The only thing to do if that happens is to push in the clutch pedal, thus disconnecting the drive, brake the car to a stop using gradual pressure on the brake pedal with your right foot, and try again. After several attempts, you will find yourself getting the knack of judging the point at which the clutch begins to engage and the correct degree of pressure to exert on the gas pedal.

Beginners sometimes find this difficult because it means they have to think of several things at once: the left foot is performing an unfamiliar manoeuvre at the same time as the right foot is going through equally unfamiliar—but different —evolutions. On top of that, both hands are engaged in tasks which are new to them and the brain has a hard time ensuring that the correct message is passed to the appropriate limb. Be comforted. When you have had sufficient practice, these movements will become automatic and this aspect of driving will not exercise your conscious mind. A common fault in the initial stages stems from over-caution. Having s-l-o-w-l-y allowed the clutch pedal to travel up to the point of gear engagement, the novice tends to snatch his foot away just as the car begins to move but before the drive has been completely taken up. A fierce leap forward is the result. Remember that the clutch pedal has a certain amount of free travel before the clutch plates actually come together. It is at the critical point of engagement that delicacy of control is needed.

Once having mastered the art of starting off smoothly, you are ready to practise moving up through the gears. Each time you progress from one gear to the next, you must depress the clutch pedal to disengage the drive and lift your foot from the gas pedal to allow the engine speed to drop. Then move the gear lever through neutral to the next position, take up the drive again by gradually releasing the clutch pedal, and increase road speed by giving the engine more gas with your right foot.

Moving Off

The car is now in motion—upwards of a ton of metal with

two people in it, rolling along at perhaps 25 miles per hour. At this juncture, knowing how to slow down or stop assumes some importance. There are several ways of doing this. You can simply take your foot off the gas pedal and allow friction between the wheels and the road surface to reduce the impetus of the vehicle. You can apply the footbrake with varying degrees of pressure to achieve gradual or rapid loss of speed. Or you can use the engine to do the work of slowing the car by changing down into a lower gear. Of these three methods, it is the last which usually gives the beginner the most trouble. We do not want to confuse him by making his first excursion at the wheel too complicated, so we will leave our description of changing down until the next chapter. Suffice it for the time being that the learner can stop the car, and quickly if necessary.

It goes without saying that your instructor will have chosen a little-frequented road for this initial foray, both to avoid as far as possible the distraction which other traffic would cause you and to save inconveniencing other drivers. As the car is fitted with dual-control, the instructor can help you out if you do something silly, but it is a mistake to rely on him to retrieve your mistakes. Just look on the dual-control as an extra brake, for use only in emergency, and learn to cope with your driving problems yourself. You are bound to make mistakes: it is only natural that you should. If it helps, remind yourself that your instructor almost certainly made just the same "boobs" as you are doing when he first learned to drive. You will learn all the more quickly through making mistakes, so they are really blessings in disguise.

All the while you have been taking the car forward at varying speeds between low and top gears, your hands will have been busy ensuring that the vehicle moves along in the required direction. We recommend choosing a straight road for the very first essay "on the move" because this enables you to concentrate on gear changing without the added distraction of steering problems. But it's a long road which has no turning and the time has come to learn how to get round corners.

Cornering

First, turning left out of the road you have previously been driving along. Let us take a straightforward 90 degree turn. You are in top gear, so you change to a lower one to reduce speed. The lower gear also gives greater control and more stability as the car takes the corner. Glance in the mirror to see what is behind and, if necessary, operate your mechanical indicators. Bear in mind there may be cyclists on your blind side and also pedestrians on the pavement who could benefit from a signal. At the same time the bad practice of swooping out towards the middle of the road before starting a turn is in all circumstances to be avoided. If changing into the lower gear has not slowed the car sufficiently, use the brake as well to bring you down to the speed at which you judge the turn

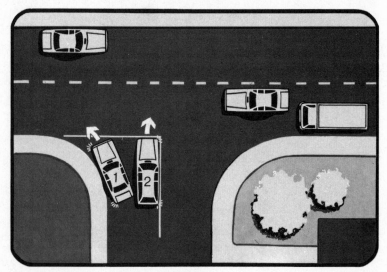

Car 1 is positioned correctly for a left turn, Car 2 for a right turn.

can be made safely.

A turn which has been made correctly will leave the car the same distance from the kerb after straightening up the wheel as it was before you turned and the vehicle should have

When turning left always take the nearside lane.

followed as nearly as possible the contour of the bend itself. Cutting the corner too sharply usually means that the car ends up too far from the kerb at the end of the turn; taking the corner too wide can inconvenience traffic approaching the junction or crossroads from your left. If you take the corner too fast, centrifugal force will throw your weight against the door and your control will be impaired. Moreover tyre adhesion, particularly if the road is wet, may be affected sufficiently to cause a skid; so take it gently until you have enough experience to judge the right speeds for negotiating differently-angled corners. We explained in an earlier chapter how the hands should be disposed on the steering wheel to give the maximum control; avoid the temptation to cross your arms when taking a particularly sharp bend.

When your instructor feels that you can make a left turn competently, he will ask you to make a right turn. Obviously, the basic procedure is similar, but you need to be more than ever careful when you perform this manoeuvre since it involves turning *across* the path of traffic coming in the opposite direction. Well before you turn right, look in your mirror to make sure you know the position and movement of traffic behind you. When it is safe give a right turn indicator signal —if you suspect this has not been seen then duplicate with a hand signal—and, as soon as you can do so safely, take up a position just left of the middle of the road or in the lane marked for right-turning traffic. If there is a white line down the middle, your offside wheels should be as near to it as possible. This is one occasion when a hand-signal is of paramount importance, though the Highway Code omits to mention it.

Another glance in the mirror keeps your brain informed about what is going on behind you, but in any event your position is such that following traffic has room to come through on your left. Once again, following the "turning drill": change down, reduce speed. The oncoming traffic may be such that you will have stopped to await your chance to cut across the road to the right. When the way is clear make your turn, as before following the contour of the bend as

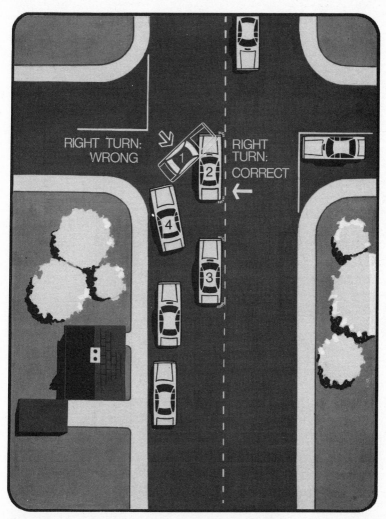

Car 1 is incorrectly positioned for a right turn, the vehicle is obsctructing Car 4 which is proceeding straight ahead. Cars 2 and 3 have taken up the correct line for a right turn.

closely as you can, so that when you straighten up you are the normal distance from the kerb. Cutting the corner when turning right is particularly dangerous because by doing so you are trespassing on road space used by oncoming traffic. When your turn is safely completed ensure that your indicator has turned to the neutral position.

Careful study of the diagrams illustrating this book will clearly confirm and even supplement what has been written in these pages.

One of the many "golden rules" in driving is, "Do not rely on signals given by unauthorized persons" and it is well to remember this particularly when turning right. Sitting in your car in the middle of the road waiting for the opportunity to make your turn, you feel horribly exposed and vulnerable. It is a temptation when some bystander waves you on, perhaps assuming a degree of skill and ability which you do not yet possess. Take no notice of this kind of gratuitous "advice". *You* are in control of the car, subject only to the emergency safeguard provided by your instructor and the dual-control device. It is *you* who must decide when it is safe to move, so, even if you have a queue of vehicles waiting behind you to follow you into the turn, ignore all well-meant efforts to do your thinking for you. Take your time and do it in safety. Practice making left- and right-hand turns continually, until your instructor is satisfied that you can do them properly.

Coming to a Halt

Earlier in this chapter we dealt briefly with the methods of bringing the car to a halt. There is more to it, however, than just putting on the brakes—or, to use the colourful language of the sporting motorist, "clapping on the anchors". More than in any other motoring manoeuvre it is important that when you slow down or stop, you should be meticulous in making your intention clear to other road users, and particularly those following behind. In bringing the car to a halt, the first and obvious action some distance from the spot at which you intend to come to rest is to remove the right foot from the gas pedal. Look in the mirror. If necessary, make the signal shown in the Highway Code "I intend to slow down or stop". Then, as your speed falls off, depress the clutch pedal and apply gradual pressure to the footbrake.

Try to judge the width of the car accurately enough to place it within six inches of the kerb when you come to a stop. This takes a little time, but trial and error will probably teach you that by lining up the bonnet *motif* or the edge of the near-side wing with some point on the kerb or pavement, you can manage it to within an inch or two. Avoid scuffing the kerb if you can, because this is liable to damage the tyres. When you have rolled to rest, apply the handbrake and then move the gear lever to the neutral position.

For your first outing you have had plenty of new experiences. Before advancing to the next stage of instruction, practise, practise, practise until you are able to perform these essential evolutions of starting, changing up, turning and stopping without the least hesitation or difficulty. The first round of your battle for control of the internal-combustion engine-driven vehicle will have been won when you have achieved this. It's not so bad or difficult as it seems really, and what fun it will be when you can drive efficiently. Keep at it!

8

Coping with Slopes

You are coming along fine. But there are still several basic skills to be acquired before you are able to make the car behave fully in accordance with your intentions. You are competent to start and stop the car on the straight and level, and you have learned how to take it round corners. The rolling English road, however, not only twists and turns from left to right, it goes up and down in a way which is often a little daunting for the learner, who has visions of the vehicle taking charge and careering away with him. In this chapter we shall deal with some aspects of controlling the car on hills. When you have got the measure of the techniques we are about to describe, you will have gone a long way towards mastery of the controls—usually the most nerve-racking time for any novice—and from here on you will probably find the remainder of your driving instruction becomes easier and easier.

For doing down hills, you must know how to change down into a lower gear so that the engine helps to brake the car, and getting the hang of changing down frequently causes the biggest headaches. The movements are simple enough—it is nervousness caused by the somewhat embarrassing jerks, jolts and loud metallic noises of a bad change-down which make it appear more difficult than it is. Make up your mind from the start that you are not going to allow yourself to get flustered.

Changing down is almost exactly the same as changing up, only, of course, in reverse. You will find it easier to start with a change from top gear to third, or (in the case of a car with only three forward gears), to second, rather than going down two gears. In the knowledge that you are about to change down, you will have steadied your foot on the gas pedal. Now push down the clutch pedal, raise your right foot from the gas pedal and put the gear lever into neutral. Then release clutch pedal (up) and down with the gas pedal to increase the engine revolutions to suit the lower gear that is coming. Next, depress (down) clutch pedal, raise (up) gas pedal and move the lever into gear. Finally, release (up) clutch pedal and down with the gas pedal again. This is the formula for double-declutching which we gave you in Chapter Four. On most gear boxes, the slight resistance which can be felt as the lever moves into the neutral position makes the pause a natural one. At this point, the car is "coasting" with the drive disconnected by the clutch, and the engine noise will be louder because you are "revving" it by keeping your foot pressed on the gas pedal. This may be disconcerting at first, but do not let it put you out of countenance. Avoid any tendency to press harder on the gas pedal. This would result in the engine racing too fast for a smooth change. You have now to take up the drive again by gradually releasing the clutch pedal, not forgetting that the greatest delicacy of control is required at the point where the gears engage. If you snatch your foot away too suddenly the car will decelerate rapidly, with a protesting howl from the transmission, and will jolt you forward uncomfortably in your seat.

Remember that when changing *up* the gas pedal comes *up* to allow the engine speed to drop; the difference when changing *down* is that the gas pedal stays *down* to maintain engine revolutions.

The better, safer motorist of today uses his gears constantly because this gives him greater control of the vehicle under varying road and traffic conditions. It is not only to slow the car that a lower gear is selected. Sometimes it is best to change down in order to obtain a short burst of speed. We will be dealing with the "when" and "why" of changing down later in the book. For the present, concentrate on mastering the "how" of changing down until you have achieved the ability to do it smoothly and effortlessly. The synchro-mesh mechanism which operates on all but first and reverse gears will prevent you from doing serious damage to the gearbox, but continual maltreatment of the gears by heavy-handed and heavy-footed driving will put a severe strain on the mechanism; this can lead to costly repairs. It is apparent, therefore, that there are several good reasons why it is important to cultivate gear-control at as early a stage as possible.

Of course, changing gear is not an end in itself: it is merely one of the means by which you are advancing towards proficiency as a driver. Make sure, therefore, that while you are learning this particular aspect of driving—or, for that matter, any other individual aspect—you do not concentrate on it to the exclusion of everything else. Do not fall into the trap of getting so wrapped up in the job of changing down, for example, that you forget for the moment what you have been taught about steering. Your left hand is busy with the gear lever and as likely as not your right hand is unconsciously dragging at the steering wheel so that the car is veering off towards the middle of the road. Your instructor will quickly draw your attention to any fault of this kind. Let it serve as a reminder that the art of driving depends on the proper co-ordination of *all* the controls.

Starting on a Hill

It would be a dull lesson without some variety, so this is a good time to try out another manoeuvre: starting from rest on a hill. By now you will have had enough experience of starting and stopping on level ground to do so with perfect ease. The hill start is a little more tricky because it calls for rather more skilful control. You must move off without allowing the car to roll backwards even an inch, and this involves doing more things at once than you have been called upon to manage up to now.

Your handbrake will at this point of course be on. Go through the normal starting drill, namely switch on, depress the clutch pedal and select first gear. Then give the gas pedal a shade more pressure than you would for moving off on the flat, to compensate for the greater load the engine has to pull. At the same time, release the clutch pedal until you feel it begin to "bite". Check in your mirror that it is safe to move off and give the appropriate signal, if necessary. At the critical point of gear engagement you must almost simultaneously: give slightly more gas; slowly release the clutch pedal so that the car strains against the handbrake; release the handbrake. The knack lies in synchronizing the release of the handbrake with the letting in of the clutch, and getting to know the right amount of pressure to exert on the gas pedal. Plenty of practice will soon teach you this.

If you find that the engine keeps stalling or that the car runs backwards, try the operation on a more gradual slope and work up from that to steeper and steeper gradients. Stalling will occur if you snatch your foot away from the clutch pedal or if you give too little gas. If the car rolls backwards it means that you are letting the handbrake off before the engine has taken the load. There is no need to panic when this happens: you stop the car when it is moving backwards in exactly the same way as you do when it is travelling forwards, by depressing the clutch and brake pedals both together. Then apply the handbrake, bring the gear lever to neutral and try again.

Once you are successfully launched on the hill you will find that your changes up through the gears have to be made much more slickly than is necessary on level ground. The car's momentum is not so great because of the gradient and consequently the next gear must be engaged quickly before the road speed falls off too much. Here your previous gear-changing experience will stand you in good stead. You may also find, if the hill is steep, that when you reach top gear the car does not respond properly and the engine labours. This means that the load is too great for the engine to carry in this gear, so you must put into practice your newly-gained knowledge and change down to third. If the hill is very steep, you may have to change yet again to second in order to find the ratio at which the engine pulls comfortably.

What goes up must come down and having at last climbed to the top of the hill you are faced with the prospect of descending it. Starting off from rest on a downward slope, compared with starting uphill, is simplicity itself, but there is a right and a wrong way of doing it. With the gear lever in neutral you have only to release the handbrake and the car will roll forward of its own accord. But remember that a car in motion with the drive disconnected is completely unstable. Poised as you are at the top of a hill in a ton of motor car, this is no situation in which to promote a lack of stability! Before letting go the handbrake therefore, select first gear. Then, just as for starting uphill, wait until the clutch pedal has reached the critical point of engagement before allowing the car to move forward. You will need little or no gas pressure, but when the car does begin to move it will be under *your* control and not under its own.

On a reasonably sharp downward gradient, you will find immediate confirmation of what we have been explaining about the use of the engine as a brake. If you leave your foot off the gas pedal and allow the car to run in first gear, you can feel the vehicle being held back and the speedometer is unlikely to rise above about 15 m.p.h. The engine is, however, being made to work unnecessarily hard. The slope is not nearly steep enough to call for the maximum braking provided by first gear, and a change up to second and probably third will be needed in order to negotiate the hill at a safe and reasonable speed. All the time your foot should be covering the brake pedal, ready to slow down if need be.

Avoiding Over-confidence

By this stage of your tuition, you will probably be congratulating yourself on the fact that you are really getting the hang of this business of driving which not so long ago seemed a formidably difficult enterprise. There's nothing wrong in that: self-confidence is an essential part of driving. But beware of over-confidence. Remember that all the driving you have done so far has been under the close supervision of your instructor and on roads carrying very little traffic. You have been concentrating, with little else to distract you, on manipulating the controls to make the car start, moving forward in different gears, turning left and right and stopping. Braking and acceleration have been simplified by the absence of other traffic.

Yet despite all these circumstances in your favour, your actions have not reached the stage where they are automatic. You have been able to stop and think, if you made a mistake or were unsure of the next move, before completing a manoeuvre. Not until the motions of driving are completely free from conscious effort is it possible for a motorist to devote his whole mind to the job of coping with the continual succession of problems which present themselves to him for decision as he drives along. A high degree of concentration is needed to receive, analyse and act upon all the messages about actual or potential hazards which reach him through his eyes and ears. So it is that the learner must stifle any delusions that he has now achieved sufficient skill to enable him to "go it alone" without any further help from his instructor. For delusion it is. Road sense is developing, there is a growing awareness of the "feel" of the car, but there is still a great deal to be learned.

9

"Do You Reverse?"

It used to be *de rigeur* in Victorian ballrooms for waltzing gentlemen to enquire of their lady partners: "Do you reverse?" The ladies appreciated this nicety because it spared them the embarrassment of unseemly stumbles if it should so happen that they had not yet learned this step in dancing class. No learner driver is likely to be asked the question in quite the same way, but reversing is nevertheless an accomplishment of which anyone will obviously find it useful to be able to boast!

The very nature of the situations in which it is necessary to drive the car backwards are such that high speeds would be out of place. Backing into a narrow entrance such as a garage doorway, for example, calls more for judgement of distance than for speed. For this reason the reverse gear has an even lower ratio than first gear. The response to pressure on the gas pedal is consequently more immediate and this means that extra fine control is required in order to avoid abrupt and uneven movements. This exercise is really only another application of clutch control which you have been practising so assiduously in the forward gears and is unlikely to cause much difficulty. For once, it is permissible to slip (feather) the clutch a little so as to maintain an even rate of travel.

To start with, try reversing in a straight line to accustom yourself to the feel of it and also to discover the best position from which you can both see and steer. The driving posture when reversing is almost invariably uncomfortable, but happily it is not necessary to drive backwards for long periods. You will probably find that the least awkward way of doing it is to twist your body sideways in the driving seat, steadying yourself by putting your left arm along the back of the passenger seat. In this way you can look over your left shoulder through the rear window and at the same time keep your right hand on the steering wheel and operate the foot controls without performing extravagant contortions. It is a mistake to rely on the driving mirror when reversing: you generally want to place the car within fairly close limits and a reflected image is a poor substitute for direct vision.

It is rarely necessary to reverse far in a straight line—indeed the law, although imprecise on the point, forbids reversing for more than a "reasonable" distance. More often than not, reversing is combined with a change of direction. Steering in reverse is simple. You move the steering wheel in the same direction that you wish the *tail* of the car to move. Turn the wheel to the right and the tail goes right; turn it to the left and the tail goes left.

When you wish to reverse to the right, it is simpler as a rule to look backwards by putting your head out of the side window rather than looking through the rear window. Whichever way you wish to turn, start by holding the steering wheel with your free hand at the "12 o'clock" position to give yourself the maximum amount of turn in one movement. If you are so built that you can keep both hands on the steering wheel, all the better: two hands are always better than one where steering is concerned.

Now try a complete turnabout in the road. First, naturally, make sure that no vehicles are either behind you or in front of you. Slow right down, (changing down, of course); signal if necessary; and then turn the steering wheel as far as it will go to the right. When the front wheels of the car have reached a point about a yard from the kerb on the opposite side of the road, by which time you will be moving very slowly indeed, turn the steering wheel to the left as far as it will go. You have only about two feet in which to do this—*without* crossing your arms, remember?—because you *must* stop the car before it touches the kerb. Apply the handbrake, otherwise the camber will cause the car to roll forward.

Select reverse gear, check again that the road is clear and wait until the gear "bites" before releasing the handbrake. When you move backwards the tail will go left because you have already set the front wheels to move the car in that direction. Again slow right down to a crawl a short distance from the kerb and apply the opposite lock to the steering before coming to a stop. The road is still clear, so you can engage first gear, release the handbrake and drive off, regaining the left-hand side of the road. If the road is particularly narrow, you may not be able to complete this manoeuvre in three movements. In that case, repeat the procedure as often as is necessary.

Reversing into a Side-turning

Although it is sometimes possible to turn right round in the road in the way we have just described, it is not always necessary to do so and it is often safer as well as more convenient to use a side-turning. A side-road or driveway either to the left or to the right of a main road will do. If the turning is on the left, bring the car to a stop at least a car's length beyond it. When reversing, observe the same "turning drill" as you do when you go round a corner forwards, namely follow the contour of the bend as closely as you can, so that when you straighten up the steering again, the car is only a short distance from the nearside kerb. Be particularly careful to ensure, before you start to move back, that there is no vehicle or pedestrian behind you, and *always*, when reversing, remember that small children and animals are difficult and sometimes impossible to see through the rear window. If you notice children on the pavement when you pull up preparatory to reversing, make sure that they are out of harm's way before you move.

To make use of a side-road on the right, gain the centre of the road in just the same way as if you were going to make a normal right-hand turn. Then, assuming the road is clear,

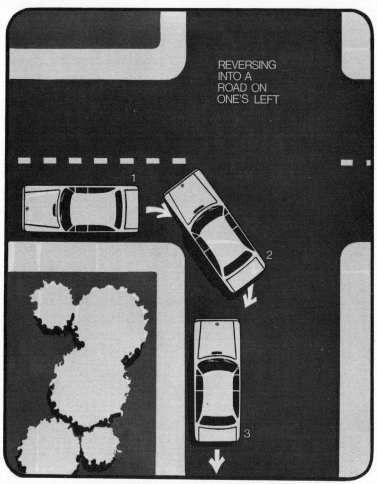

REVERSING INTO A ROAD ON ONE'S LEFT

Stop a few feet beyond the turning, not too close to the kerb. Look over left shoulder and assess the turn. As you enter junction begin to straighten steering, line car parallel to kerb and stop 12 inches from kerb. Make sure it is clear before moving back—reverse very slowly and turn steering wheel to the left.

pull across to the right-hand side, stopping close to the kerb beyond the turning. As you travel past the mouth of the side-road, assure yourself that there is no traffic approaching the junction. When the road is clear in front of you, begin reversing slowly, looking over your right shoulder to make sure that the way is still clear behind you and turning the steering wheel to the right so that your tail moves in close to the kerb on the right-hand side of the main road. Bear in mind that when the car is taken backwards, the front wheels pivot round in a wide arc, so that unless you co-ordinate your steering and accelera-tion correctly, the bonnet will swing out too far into the main road—watch this carefully. Continue to reverse well back on the right-hand side of the side-road and then stop, look behind and in front and, *if* clear, drive forward and regain the left-hand side of the side-road.

Whatever you do, never reverse from a side-road into a main road, or for that matter from your own front gate into a main road. Sticking the rear end of a vehicle into the line of passing traffic before you are in a position to be absolutely sure that nothing is coming is just asking for trouble. If you wish to turn round on a busy road it is best to go on to the next roundabout or use a side-road—in other words do your turn away from the main traffic stream.

Parking

Having learned the rudiments of reversing in relatively un-confined spaces, you are all set to tackle the much more skilled task of parking in a limited area. Traffic being what it is these days, with resultant competition for precious parking accom-modation, the area available is likely to be extremely limited and ability to make use of a minimum of space will amply compensate for time spent on practising this manoeuvre.

Because expensive mistakes are all too easy to make in the initial stage of instruction, it is not a bad idea to start by placing markers in the road to represent the tail end of one car and the front bumper of another. An expert reckons to be able to get into any space which gives him 18 inches leeway at each end of his vehicle, although this does depend to some extent on the make of car and particularly the overhang and the range of the steering lock. Learners need not think they are making things too easy for themselves if they allow a rather wider margin than this.

Forget any idea of going into a confined space front first. It won't work. If you try it, you will end up with the tail end of the car sticking out ignominiously into the path of passing traffic and no amount of shunting to and fro will improve matters. Always *back* into a tight space. First, draw up alongside and parallel with the car in front of the vacant place, after having signalled your intention to "slow down or stop". If it is left-hand reverse, apply pressure gingerly to the gas pedal while you pull the steering wheel down to the left with your right hand, and move into the space at an angle of about 45 degrees. When you judge that your nearside rear wheel is about a foot from the kerb, stop. Check that the front of your car has room to clear the rear of the vehicle in front. Then swing the bonnet slowly inwards by turning your steering wheel to the right as you continue backing gently. Properly executed, this manoeuvre should bring the car to a halt parallel with the kerb and about three inches away from it. If you get it right first time, it is a fluke! If you can manage it successfully three times out of four after a fair amount of practice, you can be fairly satisfied with your achievement.

Only when you can confidently size up an empty space with your eye and back into it competently without one false move will you be able to claim that you are a park-master.

The secret of accurate reversing is to carry out the manoeuvre slowly—remember the saying "slowly, slowly catchee monkey".

10

————◆◆◆————

Baptism by Traffic

So far you have been concentrating on learning merely how to control the vehicle. Now you are about to begin your instruction in the real art of driving—how to cope with the problems which present themselves when you take the car into traffic, baptism in fact. The techniques are not difficult to master, but they must be learnt, and learnt from experience.

Driving in traffic calls for discipline of a high order; fortunately a highly-developed sense of discipline is one of our national characteristics, otherwise driving in Britain would soon become impossible. There are more vehicles for every mile of road in our tight little island than in any other country in the world, so the ability to be in the right place at the right time, a valuable enough attribute in any sphere, assumes even greater significance when you are called upon to negotiate the many hazards of a normal car journey.

At this stage of your instruction, your basic skill in controlling the vehicle must be taken for granted. Your instructor will not allow you to mingle with the traffic stream unless he is completely satisfied on that point. Obviously he will not tax your abilities too far to start with so that you will not be "thrown in at the deep end" by being expected to tackle really dense traffic straight away.

Now you will begin to understand why we have stressed so often the need to practise the techniques of the controls until they have become automatic. There is enough to think about, you will discover, without having to worry about the physical actions necessary to move the car in the direction you want it to go. From the driving seat, you will also find that you "see more of the game" than you ever did as a passenger. You are acutely conscious of pedestrians, cyclists, traffic signs and signals, parked vehicles, oncoming traffic and following traffic. You will develop sharpened senses which will transmit a constant stream of messages to your brain and so enable you to make decisions well in advance of the actions you eventually take.

One of the first things to acquire is a sense of acceleration. It is one thing to proceed in solitary state along a deserted by-road: quite another to take station in a stream of vehicles whose speeds may vary considerably. Above all, you must learn how to position the car so as to give you the maximum forward vision. Get into the habit of dividing the road ahead of you into zones of safety and zones of danger.

Seeing Ahead

One golden rule in driving is, "If you don't know, don't go". If you can see ahead and to the left and right, you are in a position to make up your mind whether it is safe to continue. If you can't see, you don't know, so don't go. The closer you are behind the vehicle in front, the less you can see and the less safe is your driving. If you approach a blind corner, slow right down until you can see round it. If a large lorry blocks your view to the front, it is unsafe to overtake it until you can see that the road ahead is clear. Commonsense, you say? Sir or Madam, the art of driving is nothing else but applied commonsense.

There are all sorts of aids to obtaining maximum vision apart from looking straight past the end of your nose at what is going on immediately in front of you. On a curving country road, you can often see traffic approaching a long way ahead by looking over the top of the hedges. In built-up areas, you can frequently spot vehicles coming from the side by reflec-

tions in shop windows. Train yourself to such an acute awareness of what is happening around you that you are never
caught unprepared for the next move, whether it be to
accelerate, turn or slow down.

Overtaking improperly is one of the most frequent causes
of accidents and the fault is almost always in the lack of
sufficient vision. It goes without saying that you must never
overtake unless there is ample room to do so without causing
oncoming vehicles to swerve or brake. You must also never
overtake when approaching a crossroads (*because you can't
see*), or near the brow of a hill (*because you can't see*), or on a
left-hand bend (*because you can't see*), or when approaching
a pedestrian crossing (because a pedestrian about to cross
may be masked by the vehicle you are overtaking and *you
can't see*). Generally speaking, you overtake only on the right.
The exceptions to this are when a vehicle in front has taken up
position on the crown of the road to turn right, in one-way
streets and at roundabouts.

On the relatively quiet roads which have been chosen for
your first excursion in traffic, you are unlikely to meet with
many of the more sophisticated traffic control devices such as
traffic light filters, multiple roundabouts, flyovers, under-
passes and so on, which have been introduced to unravel the
tangles into which drivers are apt to get themselves in busy
town centres. But you will be confronted with enough hazards
to give you an appreciation of the need to anticipate your next
move well in advance and to adjust your driving to the pre-
vailing conditions. You are bound to come across parked
vehicles, for example, and since you will have been keeping
well in to the nearside of the road to allow other drivers to
overtake if they wish, you have to move out on to the crown
of the road in order to get past the obstructions. Following
drivers will probably know that you are about to do so
because they can see through your rear window. What they
don't know, until you tell them, is *when* you propose to pull

out. The man behind may think he can get past you before you move out, so give an indicator signal in plenty of time and drive round the parked vehicle in a gentle arc, regaining the nearside without any abrupt swerving.

Overtaking

When preparing to overtake a moving vehicle, do not move up close behind in echelon. If the vehicle in front has to stop quickly, you may not be able to pull up in time to avoid ramming into the back of it, and in any case it means that you have to strain your neck to peer round at the road ahead. Stay far enough back to give yourself adequate braking distance in emergency and to enable you to get a clear sight of oncoming traffic without performing gymnastics more appropriate to Eastern dancing ladies. Remember that if the driver in front "waves you on", and he shouldn't because there is no such signal in the Highway Code, it is entirely up to you to decide when it is safe to go past. If you are in the least doubt, if you feel that your ability to judge the speed of distant oncoming traffic is not yet sufficiently developed, then stay where you are until you are confident that it is safe for you to overtake. If in doubt—do not overtake (Highway Code). When you at last overtake pull back in front of the vehicle you have over-taken only when you are sure there is plenty of clearance—cutting-in is bad-mannered driving, and dangerous, too.

Depending on circumstances, it may be necessary to change down to the next lower gear in order to overtake—for instance when you want to overtake a long goods vehicle or a bus, particularly on a slope. This gives you a burst of speed so that you can get past more quickly and consequently reduces the amount of time when you are occupying the "danger area", i.e., the road space used by traffic travelling in the opposite direction. It follows that your gear-changing must be slicker, and you should have made up your mind that you were going to change well before your hand actually moved towards the gear lever. This is planning.

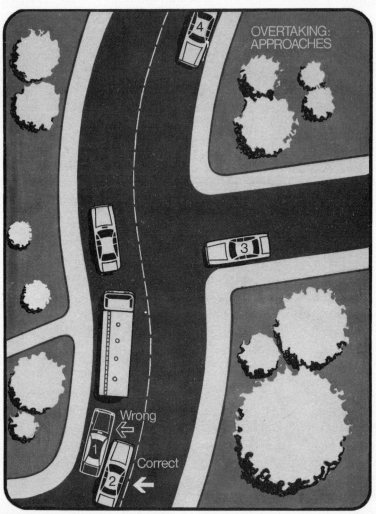

Car 1 is badly positioned, the driver is unable to see the approaching Car (4).
Car 2 is correctly positioned, the driver has a clear view of Cars 3 and 4.

Roundabouts

The Ministry gives the following useful advice on the procedure to be adopted at roundabouts:
    Unless the approach road and the roundabout itself are clear, or local conditions or road markings indicate otherwise, you should:

Turning Left—Approach in the left-hand lane; keep to that lane in the roundabout and leave by that lane. Use the left-hand indicator on approach and through the roundabout.

Going Forward—Approach in the left-hand lane; keep in that lane in the roundabout. Use the left-turn indicator at the exit before the one to be taken. If conditions dictate, approach in the right-hand lane; keep to that lane in the roundabout. Use the left-turn indicator at the exit before the one to be taken.

Turning Right—Approach in the right-hand lane; use right-hand indicator before entering roundabout and maintain this signal while keeping to right-hand lane in roundabout; change to left-hand indicator at the exit before the one to be taken.

When going forward or turning right, leave roundabout in left-hand lane of exit road unless conditions dictate use of right-hand lane. At all roundabouts give way to traffic already in the roundabout unless (in exceptional cases) road markings indicate otherwise. When in a roundabout a driver should be prepared for vehicles to cross his path in order to leave by the next exit and should be alert for any signals indicating this intention.

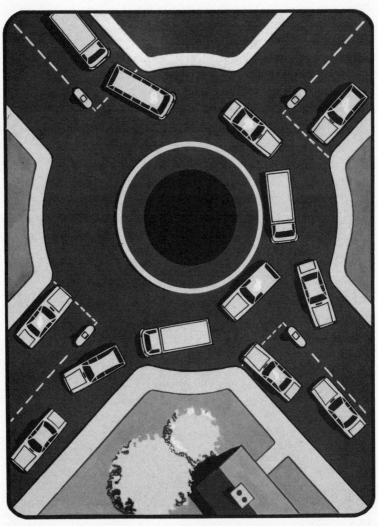

The purpose of a roundabout is to keep traffic flowing at busy intersections and when traffic is heavy it is essential to keep it moving on the roundabout itself. The broken white line facing a driver means "Give way to traffic approaching from your right".

Turning Right in Traffic

You may find that turning right at a busy crossroads is rather more confusing than it was when you first learned this manoeuvre without the distraction of other traffic. You have positioned yourself on the left-hand side of the centre line of the road so that following vehicles going straight on can filter through on your left. But approaching you in the opposite direction is a car which also wants to turn to *his* right. At first sight, it looks as though the pair of you are about to tie yourselves in a lover's knot! Do *not* try to move across in front of him. If you do that, your view of traffic coming towards you will be obstructed and you will be forced to stick your bonnet into a zone of danger where *you can't see*, thereby offending against the golden rule. The correct procedure is to drive through to the middle of the crossroads and pass *behind* the other vehicle when it is safe.

Watch out for box junctions which have criss-cross yellow lines painted on the road. Do not enter the box junction if your exit road or lane from it is not clear. But you may enter the junction when you want to turn right and are prevented from doing so only by oncoming traffic.

Pedestrians Crossing

It is unlikely that you will travel far along any road before you come to a zebra crossing. Here pedestrians have absolute precedence and it is an offence not to stop for anyone using the crossing. If there is a central island, each half of the crossing is treated as a separate entity, so that if a pedestrian has stepped off the pavement on the far side of the road when you are already close to the black-and-white markings, it is quite in order for you to go on. Make special allowance for old people and for children. The elderly are not so spry as they were and the youngsters are sometimes all too agile. Both are liable to miscalculate the speed and distance of your approaching car and you must be alert to do their thinking for them. Remember too that although all motorists are pedestrians, all pedestrians are not necessarily motorists, so they may lack appreciation.

Sudden Braking

It is not only at regulated crossing places that you need to be on the look-out for the unexpected emergency. More often than you might think a child will dash into the road after a ball, heedless of traffic, or a dog will stray oblivious of danger; these are only two of many incidents which may call for sudden braking on your part. So you must know how to perform an emergency stop. When you apply the brakes in a hurry, there is always the likelihood of a skid if the wheels become locked completely. A surface of loose gravel or chippings, or particularly, a wet or greasy road will cause this. It is just as likely to happen on a perfectly dry road which has been polished smooth by constant heavy traffic. If you have to brake hard to avoid anything which appears suddenly in your path, you will automatically depress the clutch pedal at the same time so that the engine does not continue to pull.

Only experience will tell you the amount of brake pressure you can apply without causing a skid, and when you are practising you would be well advised to choose an exceptionally quiet road preferably with an upward slope which will lessen the risk of any loss of control. Your instructor will for once tell you not to concern yourself with signals or even with the ritual glance in the mirror, although in practice you should always try to give warning to traffic behind so that they do not run into the back of your car. For sudden braking, it is also important if possible to keep the front wheels straight.

If the wheels are turned, the back of the car is likely to slew round and this will probably result in loss of control.

Given intelligent anticipation and a proper regard for the rights of other road users, you should not often be required to jam on the brakes, because normally you will always be travelling at such a speed that you can pull up before you reach a hazard. Life, however, is all too full of surprises but you can mitigate their effects if you know what to do when they arrive. Above all, never panic.

11

More About Traffic

When you have overcome any initial nervousness about driving in light traffic—and you will find it doesn't take as long as you probably feared to get accustomed to it—your instructor will let you try your hand at the wheel on more congested roads.

Here you will have to devote every last atom of concentration to the job in hand because vehicles are travelling in much closer proximity to each other and you will need to be able to position your car to much finer limits than are necessary on the open road. Here, too, you will learn that the give and take of considerate drivers helps more, perhaps, than anything else to keep traffic moving smoothly. There will be many occasions when, according to the strict letter of the rules of the road, you have the right of way, but where it is courteous, and indeed good commonsense, always waive it in favour of another road-user. Without this attitude of consideration for other road-users, the complete stagnation on the roads, which all the pundits are forever prophesying, would very soon be with us.

Practical Courtesy

Take any busy main road leading into a town centre during the morning or evening peak periods, for example. For anything up to two hours, there will be a continuous nose-to-tail procession of cars, lorries, vans and motor cycles, scooters and cyclists too, all in an orderly queue which moves at varying speeds from slow to very slow. It rarely moves fast, but it also seldom stops altogether for long. By the book, traffic on the main road has priority, so how on earth can traffic emerging from side-roads which are not controlled by light signals or a point-duty policeman expect to get into or across the stream? Vehicles can do so only if drivers on the main road are courteous enough to give way for them. That obviously doesn't mean that every time you see a car waiting to come out of a side turning, you have to stop and let him through. But if there is a reasonable gap between you and the vehicle in front, it costs you nothing to slow down, letting him know that you propose to make way for him by means of your hand signal (I intend to slow down or stop). This applies particularly if you are in a stop-start queue which is moving forward only a few yards at a time. Imagine how irritated *you* would be if you were in another driver's place and found your exit balked by a stationary vehicle in these circumstances.

Lane Discipline

Consideration for others is the whole secret of town driving and in order to practise it you must develop a keen sense of positioning. The more common expression for this is lane discipline. Many city streets are marked off into separate lanes by white lines, but, whether the lines are there or not, traffic keeps to recognized lanes which all experienced drivers understand. In very narrow streets, there is room only for vehicles moving in Indian file, but most main roads are wide enough for at least two lines of traffic in each direction. Approaches to large junctions often have three or even four lanes and in these cases the authorities usually help drivers by painting large white directional arrows on the carriageway to indicate the direction which traffic should follow.

Generally speaking, you should keep to the nearside lane—that is, within about two feet from the kerb—for most of the time. When you approach a light-controlled intersection you must get into the appropriate lane well in advance according to the direction you intend to take. If you want to turn left, you obviously remain in the nearside lane. Equally obviously, if you want to turn right you must get into the offside lane in plenty of time. If you want to go straight on, you have a choice of either the left-hand or the right-hand lane and it depends largely on the character of the crossroads which lane is best to select. If, for some reason, you were already in the right-hand lane when you came up to the intersection, it is better to stay there rather than change over to the inside lane. This means that if one or more vehicles in front of you want to turn right, you may be held up behind them and you will very probably miss the lights. On the other hand, you will have avoided the necessity of insinuating your vehicle into a stream of traffic coming through on the inside, which can be a difficult operation and almost invariably depends upon some-one giving way to you. If you are already in the left-hand lane, or can get there without undue difficulty, so much the better, because from this position you have an uninterrupted view of the road ahead once you are clear of the traffic which is actually at the crossing.

Sometimes, at a traffic intersection, congestion becomes so acute that vehicles in both directions are practically at a stand-still. When one stream gets the green light, it can move forward only for a very short distance. This is another instance where commonsense and consideration for others comes into play. If the tail of the last vehicle across has only just cleared the crossing, you will block the intersection with your car if you assert your "right of way" and go forward. Let the lights change to red again, and wait through several changes if necessary, until you can clear the crossing without obstructing the path of vehicles on the other road. What will you have lost? In time, nothing, because you would have had to wait in any case behind the car in front.

When driving in busy town streets, you will notice that vehicles follow each other much more closely than they do on the open road. While your main concern is with what is going on in front of you, it is also essential to use your mirror frequently so that you have a fairly continuous picture of the traffic scene behind you as well. This information is especially important if you decide that you want to change from one lane to another. Having made up your mind to do so, give a clear signal (you should know which one), glance in your mirror to make sure that no following vehicle is moving into the area of road you wish to occupy, and then turn positively, but not sharply, into the lane you have chosen. Never drive along in a position which is straddling both lanes. If you do, you will be displaying very bad manners indeed to drivers who are keeping their correct lanes behind you. This also applies at traffic lights: if you pull up in the middle of the road you are taking up space which two vehicles could occupy, and in cases where there is a filter-arrow allowing left-turning vehicles to proceed, you will prevent traffic from going through.

Although you are expected to leave a reasonably small gap between your own car and the vehicle in front when travelling in a stream, it is possible to overdo this. It would be foolhardy to glue yourself so closely to the man in front that you would be unable to avoid hitting him if he stopped suddenly for any reason. In just the same way, it is bad practice to close up tight to a car which has halted on an upward slope. The driver's ability to move off from rest on a hill without running backwards may not be all that it should be, and the tinkle of head-lamp glass falling on to the road is not pleasant music to hear.

Pedestrians in Heavy Traffic

Pedestrians are at a particular disadvantage when traffic is heavy, so, remember that you are a pedestrian yourself when you are not at the wheel of the car and observe the well-tried formula: "do as you would be done by". If you are in a bumper-to-bumper queue of vehicles and come to a pedestrian crossing, don't pull up so close to the vehicle in front that you are obliged to halt on the crossing itself. Again, it costs you nothing to stop in advance of the crossing—when the stream moves forward again you will easily catch up. Watch out for pedestrians all the time, and especially when overtaking parked cars or buses which are disgorging passengers. Get into the habit of glancing at the road underneath stationary vehicles. You can often get advance warning that somebody is about to step out in front of you by spotting feet when the rest of the body is hidden. Be prepared, too, when turning left at a light-controlled intersection, for pedestrians who may have stepped off the kerb to go across "with the lights". The Highway Code says that you must give way to them.

Obstruction

Parking in towns is nowadays controlled almost every-where, with varying degrees of restriction, but even where there is no prohibition you are expected to show proper consideration for others. The law of obstruction is not very clearly defined, but if you leave your car in a place where it causes inconvenience to moving traffic, you must not be sur-prised if you find yourself in trouble with the police, and possibly put to the pain of collecting the car from a police pound to boot! It is also illegal to park inside the metal studs which are fixed in the road at a distance of usually, 15 yards in front of a pedestrian crossing. The reason for this is simply that stationary vehicles in this area would obstruct the view of passing drivers, to the danger of people walking across. Unless the street is very wide and there is specific permission to park on both sides, you should also refrain from parking opposite another stationary vehicle, thus reducing the amount of space available for moving traffic. Stopping on or close to a bus stop, on or near corners and traffic lights, are other "don'ts" which you must observe meticulously.

Reading the Road

When you made your first forays into traffic you will have become familiar with many of the roadside signs, which are there to give you either information or instructions. You will undoubtedly have encountered a "Halt" sign surmounted by an inverted red triangle in a red circle as a sign of danger, and your instructor will have made sure that you did in fact bring the car to a dead stop as the law requires. Your study of the Highway Code will have prepared you to meet many other different roadside signs whose meanings you should make sure you thoroughly understand. In towns, you will meet with a great many more signs than on the open road and they will crop up at much more frequent intervals.

You must get used to taking in the information or instructions they contain almost subconsciously, and a good way to do this, paradoxically, is to start by being self-conscious about it. Give yourself a running commentary, aloud if you like but silently if you prefer, on your own driving performance and the hazards you are preparing to cope with. A typical "programme" might go something like this: "I am now approaching the outskirts of a built-up area. I can see the 30 m.p.h. speed limit sign ahead, so I am slowing down to the proper speed. There is a large van in front, travelling very slowly but I cannot overtake him yet because I have just passed a sign which tells me there is a sharp left-hand bend coming up. As the road surface is dry and affords good braking I am leaving a gap of at least three car-lengths between us so that when we come to a straight stretch of road I shall be able to see past the van without difficulty. Mirror.

"There is a car behind me which has moved over to the outside lane. I think it would be unsafe for him to pass me at this point and he appears eager to do so, but it is not for me to give him instructions so I am resisting the temptation to 'wave him back', as I have sometimes seen other drivers do. Besides, he may intend to turn into that gateway on the right—yes he is now giving the hand signal to show that he is slowing down and his right indicator is winking. Just in case he *did* start to overtake me, however, in which case he would very probably have had to cut in sharply in front of me to avoid oncoming traffic, I was anticipating that I might have to brake and I moved in as close as I could to the kerb.

"Now the road is straightening out and I can see that there is nothing coming in the opposite direction for a good distance. But I can see a flashing Belisha beacon ahead and we have just passed a 'School' sign. The van is blocking my view of the nearside pavement. There may be children about to cross. I don't know, so I don't go. Now we are past the crossing, and it is still clear to overtake. Mirror. All clear behind. Hand signal. More gas, pull out. The van driver is 'waving me on' but I am not accepting his unauthorized signal. I check for myself—it is clear and I go. Mirror. My tail is well clear of the van, so I can get back into the nearside lane.

"Traffic lights ahead, showing red. Change down. There's the red-and-amber, but wait until the green before accelerating again. Now we're coming to a roundabout and I'm taking the right-hand exit. Mirror. Signal. Move to the crown and change down. There's another car coming in from the left and it looks as though he'll get there first. Slow right down to let him through and anyway I saw a pedestrian crossing on the exit I shall be taking, with some people about to cross, so I shall need to stop

"Here's a good clear stretch so I can get up more speed. But there's a dog running loose on the pavement and it may dash into the road. I keep it in the corner of my eye, anticipate a possible emergency stop and check in the mirror to see what's behind. Dog-danger over, now here's a sign with one arrow pointing up and another pointing down. 'Two-way traffic', it says—there's plenty of room for three lanes of vehicles, but I stick to the nearside. Cyclist ahead, wobbling a bit. Mirror. Prepare to give him a wide berth. . . ." And so on.

By turning yourself into an amateur commentator in this way, you get into the habit of registering mentally all the signs, both the obvious ones and the more subtle ones, which enable you to "read" the road in front of you. This is a method which is adopted at the Police Driving Schools where some of the country's most skilful drivers are trained. After a time, you will discover that this rather self-conscious procedure has developed into an unconscious habit. When that happens, you will be well on the way to becoming a pretty competent driver yourself.

Don't worry about this commentary, it isn't half as difficult as it sounds.

12

---•◆•---

The Open Road

The joys of the open road! For most learner drivers, this is the lure which sustains them through their early struggles to master the motor car, and now at last we are off on a jaunt into the country. In the previous chapter we stressed the need for strict concentration because of the closer proximity of vehicles to each other in built-up areas than is the case on the open road. That does not mean that in the country you can "take things easily" by slacking off your effort of concentration. For one thing, vehicles are able to move more quickly and this means that your reactions must be proportionately more rapid. Moreover speed introduces problems which you will not have encountered in the driving lessons you have had so far. It is not suggested that you are ready yet for high speeds—that phase of yo'r driving experience is still some way off—but you must learn to control the car at speeds in the middle range which are normally maintained outside built-up areas.

Influence of Camber

When you are driving around in a town, you barely notice the camber of the road but at speeds above about 30 m.p.h. (and even, sometimes below it), the angle of camber can have a marked effect on the steering. You must now learn to scan the surface of the road ahead all the time so that you are prepared to counteract the "pull" which you can feel on the steering wheel. This is particularly important when you take a right-hand bend because a combination of centrifugal force (which is tending to make the car continue its original line of travel) and the camber (which is bodily tilting the car in the same direction) can land you in difficulties if you are unprepared for it and you are going too fast.

"Coming unstuck" or "running out of road" are the light-hearted expressions used by the motor racing fraternity for an experience which can be the far-from-amusing result of attempting to take a bend with the "wrong" camber at too great a speed. Of course, not all right-hand bends have the "wrong" camber, i.e., tilting outwards. Many of them are "super-elevated" by being slightly banked inwards and have what road engineers call a "built-in speed factor"—they are calculated to allow vehicles to drive round safely up to a given maximum speed.

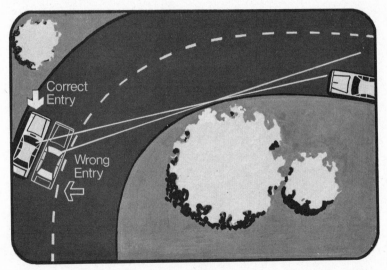

The driver of the correctly positioned car has a clear view of the approaching vehicle and is not cutting the bend.

On a left-hand bend, the camber produces the same effect as super-elevation and helps the driver to get round more

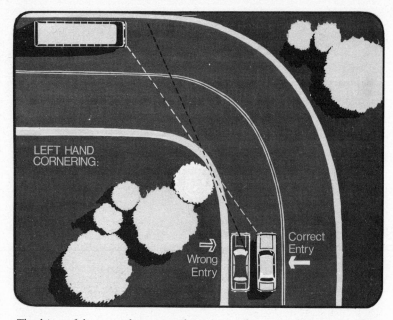

LEFT HAND
CORNERING:

Correct
Entry

Wrong
Entry

*The driver of the correctly positioned car can see the approaching coach and has
plenty of time to regain the nearside on the apex of the bend.*

easily, but left-hand bends, particularly in narrow lanes
bordered by high hedges, carry their own dangers through
lack of visibility. One of the temptations in a situation of this
kind is to move out as far as possible to the centre of the road
to obtain a better view. Resist it at this stage. The safe way to
negotiate a bend of this nature is to slow down sufficiently
to enable you to stop if you come across an obstruction such
as a farm cart or a flock of sheep in your path. On the crown
of the road you are vulnerable to any on-coming vehicle
which may be approaching at speed and with its offside wheels
on your side of the white line.

Accelerating on a Curve

When you are taking a curve which provides you with ample

forward visibility, remember that much greater stability is achieved under acceleration than under deceleration. Slow down, therefore, before you enter the turn (and change down if necessary), then accelerate gently as you go round.

Try to judge the correct amount of braking to apply so that when you begin to turn the steering wheel, your foot has left the brake pedal and you are preparing to give more gas. When you have done this a few times you will discover that the "feel" of the car as it moves round a bend under acceleration is much more positive than it is if you react too late and continue braking on the bend itself. Instead of being in a "nose-down" attitude caused by the car's retardation, your pressure on the gas pedal is making the driving wheels push you round. The operation of the differential is turning the rear wheel on the inside of the curve slower than the driving wheel on the outside.

Your constant scanning of the road surface will give you other indications which will enable you to prepare well in advance to adjust your steering to conditions. When you come to a stretch where there is a change in the colour of the surfacing material, you can expect a jolt on the steering wheel where the join is a little uneven, and will have anticipated this by steeling your grip on the wheel. Similarly potholes or sunken manhole covers can throw the steering out of true unless you are prepared for them.

Crossroads and Signs

On quiet rural roads you will frequently come across uncontrolled crossroads. Treat them with as much circumspection as you would treat an intersection in a town which is not governed by traffic lights. Slow right down, sound your horn, and go across only when you can see that there is nothing coming in either direction. Watch for a head over the hedge, it may be a cyclist. Just because you have had the road to yourself for miles, you must never assume that yours is the only vehicle on the road.

Some of the road signs you will see on your country excursion are not so often met with in towns. The "clearway" sign, for example, which is followed by "repeater" signs at regular intervals to act as reminders, means that you must not stop on the carriageway. In any case it is always safer for you, and displays good manners towards others, to pull off the road into a lay-by or on to the verge, whether the road is a "clearway" or not. If the road is twisting and narrow, there will probably be double white lines, or a combination of double- and dotted-white lines. There are many more of these on country roads than in towns. To disregard them is an offence, and is fool-hardy too. The lines are laid down to a set formula and are designed to do some of your thinking for you. If we were all perfect drivers with impeccable judgement, there would be no need for the double white line system, because we should all automatically position our vehicles in such a way that we would not encroach on a zone of danger. Bitter experience has shown the authorities that it is safer to give drivers clear-cut instructions which eliminate the possibility of error of judgement.

The cattle-crossing sign in the shape of a cow in silhouette, the omega-shaped sign of a hump-backed bridge and the sign showing a toy train in outline which indicates a level-crossing unguarded by gates, are typical warnings you will meet on country roads and you should never treat them lightly. Nine times out of ten there will be no train in sight when you come to the level-crossing and, incidentally, the level-crossing which is really level is a rare exception, so be prepared for some violent steering judder. But you must never disregard these signs. Ease your foot off the gas pedal and prepare for a sudden stop if necessary. The ruminative beast is not renowned for its road-sense, and the railway engine has none.

Of course, not all the hazards of a drive in the country will be pointed out to you by road signs. You are likely to see fewer pedestrians but those you meet may be less prepared for traffic than the agile city-dweller. Give them a gentle toot on your horn just to make sure they know you are coming. People riding horses should be given an especially wide berth, and you should slow down more than usual when passing them. Not all horses display the imperturbability of the London police horse which is specially trained to traffic, and if you roar past or cut too close you easily may cause them to shy and throw their riders. Dogs and cats in the country are not likely to show the same qualities of road-sense that their town-bred cousins seem to acquire, and they, too, should be treated warily.

Just as in town driving, you must keep a good look-out as far ahead as possible and to your left and right so that your eyes constantly take in and transmit to the brain a composite picture of what is happening now and what is likely to happen next. You may be surprised to discover how your heightened perceptions will enhance your enjoyment of the country scene. But *never* take anything for granted.

13

——•••••——

Night Driving

Although this book is intended as a manual for the learner driver, who will naturally have his ambitions fixed on the goal of passing the driving test, we have not by any means set out to write a "driving text crammer". The aim is to teach the novice the art of better, safer motoring today step by step so that he cultivates the correct method of car control in a way which will serve as a solid foundation of training when he moves on to advanced driving lessons at a later stage. Night driving is not normally included in the curriculum of driving schools because the majority of beginners want to take their instruction under exactly the same conditions as they will experience when they go for their test, and all tests are conducted in daylight. Sooner or later, however, and especially in the winter months when the hours of daylight are so short, the pupil will be faced with the necessity of driving after dark.

Checking Lights

Just as in daylight you must always travel at such a speed that you can pull up within the distance you can see to be clear, so at night you must always keep within the braking range of your headlights. It follows, therefore, that your lights must all be in good working order and that the headlamps must be properly aligned. Get into the habit before driving off at night of checking the lights by switching them on and then walking round the car to satisfy yourself that both tail lamps and both sidelights are functioning. Switch on the headlights and operate the dip-switch, but wait until you are sure you will not dazzle other drivers before doing so.

Checking the operation of the stop-lights is not so easy unless you can get someone outside the vehicle to tell you that they come on when you depress the brake pedal. One way of doing this, if you are moving off from your garage at home, is to back up fairly close to the wall so that you are able to see the reflections of the light on each side. In the street, it is often possible to get a reflection in a shop window, or from the bonnet of a car parked behind you. This may sound to you like exaggerated precaution, but it is not. If you are driving along on a black night with your offside tail light not functioning, for example, a fast car coming up behind might think that the single light he can see close to the verge belongs to a motor cycle. He may have to swerve dangerously to avoid hitting you, or his reactions may not be rapid enough. . . . If one of your stop-lights does not work, or has a weak connexion so that it winks on and off when you apply the footbrake, a following driver may get the mistaken impression that you are indicating a turn, with similarly dangerous consequences. Again, if only one sidelight is in action, oncoming vehicle drivers may mistake your car for a bicycle or a motor cycle and the resultant confusion could lead to an accident. Vehicle lamps are sturdy and stand up to a lot of hard wear, but, giving no warning when they fail, they need to be checked regularly.

Town Lights

Street lighting varies enormously in towns and there may be several different types of lighting in the course of a journey of only a mile or two. Generally speaking, only main roads are sufficiently well lit for you to be able to see adequately with sidelights alone. You must use dipped headlamps at all times when the lighting is poor. This not only enables you to see better, but ensures that other road-users—pedestrians in particular—can see *you* in good time. City streets, especially when it is raining, are such a confusing mass of lights and reflections from vehicles, shop windows, traffic signals and lamp-posts that it is not easy for pedestrians to tell which is which in a few moments. There is no mistaking a car with its headlights switched on and there is no possibility of confusing it with a stationary vehicle showing only parking lights.

Your Lights and Other Cars

When travelling in a stream of traffic in circumstances where you need to use dipped headlights, do not follow too closely behind the man in front. If you do, your headlamps blazing into his rear-view mirror will dazzle him. Keep far enough behind so that your dipped beam falls just short of the rear of his vehicle and your lights will not then cause him any difficulty. Winking direction indicators, which in some cases are exceptionally brilliant, can also cause annoyance if they are used thoughtlessly, by dazzling the driver behind you when you are stationary at a junction or crossroads and waiting to make a turn. Once you have indicated the direction you intend to take and have positioned yourself in the correct lane to do so, it is pointless to sit with your indicator light blinding into the eyes of the driver who has pulled up behind you. If traffic is heavy, you may have to wait for several minutes before you are able to move off again. When you do eventually prepare to go into the turn, you can wink your indicator again as a reminder. In the meantime, you will have saved the following driver unnecessary eye-strain.

While it is permissible (though not recommended if it can be avoided) to park in the daytime facing oncoming traffic, at night YOU MUST NEVER DO SO. Once again, the reason is to avoid confusing oncoming traffic. On a black night, with no street lighting and perhaps no white road-markings or distinguishable kerb to guide him, a passing driver may be misled into thinking that the road curves sharply because your sidelights give him the impression that he is on the wrong side of the road.

On the open road, you will find that your headlights on main beam will give you ample vision ahead, particularly if there are "cat's-eyes". But remember that although the line of glinting cat's-eyes may stretch a long way into the distance, your headlights do not give you effective vision as far as that. The cat's-eyes give you a valuable foreknowledge of the direction the road is taking but they can never take the place of your lights. Remember also that while you are able to see oncoming motor vehicles a long way away, the lights of a pedal cycle rarely carry far (and, lamentably, are all too often not carried at all), while pedestrians and animals may appear in your path without warning.

Always dip your headlights to avoid dazzling drivers coming towards you. Even if, having dipped your own lights, an oncoming driver is inconsiderate enough to keep his headlamps on full beam, do not "retaliate" by flashing yours at him: the road at night is no place for an exchange of discourtesies. Show a little thought for pedestrians, too, if you meet them on a country road, and dip your lights so that they are not forced to stumble blindly into the ditch—or perilously into the road.

If you find that the lights of oncoming traffic, dipped or not, dazzle you so that you cannot see, slow down, and look away from them by casting your eyes at the nearside kerb.

Beware Twilight!

Probably the most dangerous time of all for drivers is in that twilight half-hour between daylight and dark. During this period your eyes often play tricks on you and judgement of speeds and distances can be impaired. It is not yet dark enough for your headlights to be effective but the fading daylight tends to blur outlines and throw faint shadows which can be deceptive. Use extra caution and help other drivers by switch-ing on your sidelights early. Far too many drivers still leave it until far too late before they switch on their lights. If they do that in the belief that they are saving wear on the battery they are curiously misinformed because the dynamo automatically charges at a higher rate when extra load has to be met.

After 11.30 p.m. it is against the law to sound your horn in a built-up area. You can, however, use your headlights as a warning instead. When you come to a crossroads, for in-stance, you can let traffic on the other road know you are there by flashing your headlights as you slowly approach the intersection. Watch out for the flash of light from the crossing road which is a warning from another driver that *he* is there.

Within Headlight Range

There need be no terrors for you in night driving if you observe the simple rule we gave at the beginning of this chapter, namely drive only within the range of your headlights. This automatically means that you would drive more slowly than you would, given the same road and traffic conditions, in daytime. Moreover artificial illumination is a poor substitute for natural light and you will not be able to see in such detail variations in the road surface.

Driving at night can often be more enjoyable than driving in the daytime because there is usually not so much traffic about. The danger is to become over-confident and to assume that because you appear to have the road to yourself you can "put your foot down" with impunity. The golden rule "If you don't know, don't go" still applies; be sure you can stop in the distance covered by your headlights. Look at the brak-ing-distance chart and bear in mind that at 30 m.p.h. on a *dry* road and with efficient brakes you will not be able to stop until you have travelled 75 feet and that at 50 m.p.h. you will require considerably more, namely 175 feet.

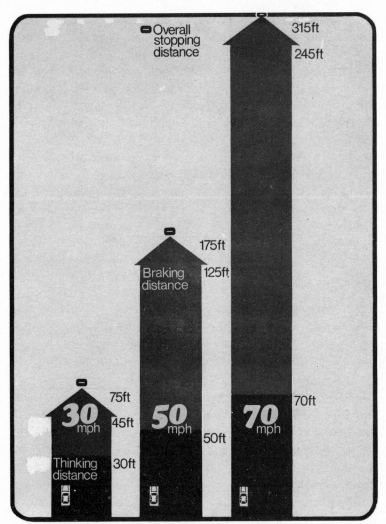

These figures are compiled on the assumption that your reaction time (thinking distance) is average and road conditions are sound thus affording good braking facilities. As one grows older extra allowance must be made for thinking distance and if the road surface is wet, greasy or covered in frost, ice, snow, mud or leaves then the braking distance obviously increases. The figures are from the Highway Code.

14

━━━━●◦●━━━━

When the Weather is Bad

You won't do much motoring in Britain if you are only a fair-weather driver. Our "temperate" climate, as the meteorologists quaintly describe it, includes a fair proportion of snow, ice, frost, fog and sleet; a good all-rounder must be a foul-weather driver, too. When you have mastered the techniques of driving in bad weather conditions described in this chapter, you must not expect to be up to Monte Carlo rally standards, but you will be equipped to cope with most of the hazards which winter brings.

Snow and Ice

Driving on snow and ice causes learners some trepidation at first and it certainly calls for extra care and concentration, but the car can be kept under perfectly safe control if you remember two cardinal rules: never brake violently and never change direction suddenly. It follows from this that your speed should be such that it is never necessary to do either of these things. All your movements must be smoother and more deliberate—your steering, your gear-changing and clutch control, your acceleration and your braking.

Above all be careful with your braking. When the road is like an ice-rink, even light brake-pressure will sometimes lock the wheels and if that happens you will simply slide forward because the tyres cannot get a grip. Use that other brake— the engine—by changing down into a lower gear. If that does not slow you down quickly enough and you are forced to apply the brakes, do so with a "pumping" action sometimes known as "dab-braking". Press the foot down on the brake pedal until you can feel that the wheels have locked, then immediately release the pedal and repeat the process. You thus obtain the maximum braking possible without locking the wheels for long enough to cause a skid. On slippery surfaces, it is also asking for trouble to brake with the front wheels turned. A skid which takes you straight forward along your original line of travel is unpleasant enough but the car is at least under partial control. If your front wheels are turned when you develop a braking skid on ice, control will go altogether and you are likely to find yourself facing the way you have come before you can say "knife".

Before setting out when the roads are covered with snow or ice, it is advisable to lower your tyre pressures by a few pounds so that there is a larger area of tyre surface to make contact with the road. It is also a sensible precaution to stow in the boot a couple of old sacks or a piece of coconut matting so that if you get stuck you can use them to give the driving wheels something to grip on. Snow chains on the rear wheels can be a help but if you do have them fitted you must not imagine that they will give you immunity from skidding. They may reduce the danger but you must still observe all the other precautions.

Probably the least hazardous of all winter weather conditions is virgin snow which has not yet been packed down by passing traffic. The fresh flakes give a relatively non-slippery surface which the tyres can grip as efficiently as on a surface which is merely wet. Before long, however, it becomes compressed into hard ruts of solid ice which need to be treated with extreme caution. If you can avoid following in these "railway lines", you will be less likely to develop a slide. Even more treacherous is an icy surface on which new snow has fallen, because the danger is hidden, so take it even more gently in these conditions.

Because friction between the wheels and the road is so much less on snow and ice, fierce acceleration will cause the driving wheels to spin. Always, therefore, drive in as high a gear as possible to reduce this risk. On a car with four forward gears, use second gear when starting off from rest and change up into top as soon as you can. Take bends and corners in as wide an arc as possible and when you approach a hill, either going upwards or downwards, change down well in advance, *double-declutching* to avoid any sudden jerks which may start a skid. If the hill is so steep that you will obviously have to make another change-down into a still lower gear, do it much earlier than you normally would so that your road speed does not fall off to such an extent that you will have to re-engage at high revolutions. Since your stopping distance is enormously increased, leave a generous gap between your car and the one in front—four or five car-lengths is not too much in towns, and on the open road, depending on the speed of the traffic stream, up to twenty car-lengths might be needed for safety.

A tip worth remembering, particularly if there is sheet-ice, which offers practically no grip for the tyres at all, is to drive with the nearside wheels running along the gully formed where the edge of the camber meets the verge. This slight channel usually has a sufficiently uneven surface to enable you to keep going. It is not often practicable to do this in built-up areas, however, because of the danger to pedestrians.

Other Dangerous Road Surfaces

So far, we have been dealing with conditions of snow and ice which, however treacherous they may be, at least have the virtue of being readily apparent. Far more dangerous are roads which have a deceptively harmless appearance, wet or dry, but which in fact present traps for the unwary. Learn to look out for small signs which will give you warning of slippery surfaces. After a spell of dry weather, for example, a light shower or even a heavy mist which merely damps the surface of the road makes the tyre marks of passing vehicles show up clearly. This is a time to be especially careful. The water combines with dust and oil spots to form a greasy film which can be every bit as slippery as ice. A good heavy downpour washes this film away, but a persistent fine drizzle which does not have the effect of "rinsing" the road can prolong the danger period for hours. Frost is usually plainly visible once it has formed, and you should treat it with the same respect that you pay to any icy road. There is, however, an interval between the time when the surface moisture begins to freeze and the appearance of the tell-tale white rime, so watch for the glint of tiny beads of water on the grass of the verge when the temperature is low.

Even on dry roads you can come across skiddy patches. In country districts you will often find stretches where mud and vegetable matter has fallen from farm vehicles. You can very easily slide on this refuse, particularly on bends. Wet leaves in the autumn also call for special care: remember that even if the leaves on top are dry, those underneath are probably wet, squelchy and dangerously slippery. A sweltering summer day which has melted tar on the road surface will provide a gooey surface on which your wheels are unable to get a proper grip. In towns, wood block surfaces or smooth stone setts call for circumspection when they are wet and you should allow for greater-than-usual braking distances.

Always drive more slowly when it is raining, and use the same technique as for driving on snow or ice: no violent movements, no heavy braking. Avoid driving through deep puddles if you can, and never try to go through them at speed. Hitting a pool of floodwater only three or four inches deep at, say, 40 m.p.h. will have much the same effect on the steering as colliding with a solid object. It is not always possible to tell from the driving seat just how deep water on the road is likely to be, so this is another reason for easing your foot off the gas pedal. If you do have to drive through floodwater watch your brakes afterwards.

All this may sound formidably difficult to the improving learner-driver. There is really nothing difficult about it: it is perfectly safe to drive in slippery conditions provided the driver is prepared for the hazards, knows how his car will react and understands what to do to maintain control of his vehicle. If you can find a *deserted* road to practise on when the snow lies (not too) deep and crisp and even, you will get a lot of fun and, even more, valuable experience by inducing a few gentle skids just to get the feel of it.

Skids

The best way to learn how to get *out* of a skid is to correct a slide which you have caused deliberately in safe circumstances like this. Make quite sure that you have the road to yourself and bring your speed to about 15 m.p.h. Then accelerate suddenly, but not so hard that your foot goes down to the floorboards. You will almost certainly find that the rear of the car slithers round to one side or the other, probably to the left because of the camber.

The first rule of skid-correction is to remove the cause of the skid, which in this case is your acceleration. Ease your foot off the gas pedal, but DO NOT TOUCH THE BRAKE. At the same time turn the steering wheel in the direction of the skid. The object is to keep the car facing in its original direction of travel. Since the back end of the car has moved in to the left, the car is now at an angle to the road with the bonnet pointing towards the opposite side, so you can now turn the steering to the left to bring the car back into line. Your heart may thump a bit the first time, but after a few more tries you will find yourself reacting naturally and deliberately and you will have gained confidence and experience which will stand you in good stead if you ever get into a skid which you are not expecting.

You can also induce a skid, of course, by braking hard on the snow-covered road. Even if your wheels are straight, the camber may slew the back of the car round, but, if the wheels are already turned, the rear end may slide away, probably in the opposite direction. Once again, the first thing to do is to remove the cause of the skid, namely the application of the brakes, simultaneously turning the steering wheel to bring you back to your original line of travel. We include this example here for instructional purposes only, however. If you drive carefully enough the occasions when you will get into a skid through braking at the wrong time should be very rare indeed.

Fog

The most frustrating of all winter ills for drivers is fog. In a real pea-souper the only thing to do is to get out and walk, because if you can't see at all you obviously can't drive at all. There are occasions, mercifully few, when even an efficient fog-lamp, properly fitted so that it directs a narrow beam of light downwards towards the kerb, cannot provide enough illumination to make driving safe. Then the golden rule applies: you don't know, so you don't go.

It is at night when fog is most troublesome, because head-lights, even in the dipped position, are prone to cause back-glare by reflection from the millions of tiny droplets of moisture. Go very slowly and bear in mind that pedestrians, because they can see you, are apt to assume that you can see them. The feeble rear light on a bicycle is even less effective than usual and it is often difficult to make out whether the stop-lights of the vehicle in front belong to a car or a lorry with a long overhang. You bless the cat's-eyes if they are there and breathe imprecations at the authorities for parsimony or neglect if they are not. Don't be so foolish as to drive along with your wheels straddling the cat's-eyes—there may be another fool coming in the opposition direction with *his* wheels straddling them too. . . .

In daytime fog, the rule is: use *dipped headlights*. You will not have any trouble with back-glare and pedestrians and other drivers will be able to see your lights before the contours of your car themselves are visible to them. Do not forget, when you park your car by the kerb, to leave your sidelights on for the benefit of others.

Remember, too, that fog has a deadening effect on sound. Pedestrians and cyclists may not hear you coming, so sound your horn frequently. Finally, keep your windscreen wipers going to clear the film of moisture which will otherwise hinder your vision. Despite all this advice, if you can avoid driving under adverse conditions do so.

15

---✦◆✦◆✦---

Road Sense and Manners

Every driver develops road sense to a greater or lesser degree. Some people have a flair for it, in the same way as a great footballer or tennis-player has a natural bent for the sport in which he excels. They are the lucky ones. For them, after they have mastered the mechanical control of the vehicle, road sense means little more than "doing what comes naturally". They improve with experience, as we all do, but the inherent ability is there. For most of us lesser mortals, whose ambition stops some way short of rivalling the heroes of the motor-racing circuit, the acquisition of road sense is a slow process which we have to cultivate consciously and assiduously.

Qualities Required in Driving

What *is* this nebulous-sounding quality which is so important in driving? It is a combination of many things and it boils down to the ability of the brain to assimilate and interpret all the information which is reaching it from various sources— from a driver's eyes and ears (and sometimes his nose), from his hands on the steering wheel, from the vibrations which are felt by various parts of his body (including the "seat of his pants" which we mentioned in an earlier chapter)—and from these to formulate a plan of action which determines the next series of movements. The brain's memory-box also comes into play so that the experience of past mistakes and successes are all taken into account. A learner-driver who has been badly

taught will develop aptitude more slowly than one who has
had the advantage of expert tuition. Professional instruction
is specifically designed to bring out the latent road sense of the
pupil and to instil in him from the outset patterns of driving
behaviour which help him to develop it naturally.

Road Sense in Action

Road sense has sometimes been described as "intuition"
or "sixth-sense". We believe this to be misleading. There is
nothing supernatural about it. If you are driving along a
perfectly straight road, for example, with nothing else about
except a solitary pedestrian harmlessly walking along the pavement some way ahead, and you experience a sense of danger
which causes you to begin braking—just in time to avoid
knocking down the walker who has suddenly stepped into the
road—that was not intuition at work. It was not even some
mysterious sixth-sense. It was your road sense in action,
triggered off by one or more of your ordinary five senses,
probably your sense of sight. Because your eyes have been
attuned to recognize the significance of everything which is
going on within their range of vision, some almost impercep-
tible movement of the head or body of that pedestrian gave
your brain the warning which caused you to brake. Your
conscious mind did not realize what was happening until after
your reflexes had taken the appropriate avoiding action.

You can often anticipate the actions of pedestrians by
studying their expressions as you approach. Take that woman
on the far pavement, for example, hurrying along with her
laden shopping baskets. She didn't exactly look round, but she
turned her head as though she was listening to hear if anything
was coming before crossing the road to the bus stop. She's
probably so busy thinking about getting home in time to give
the children their tea that she is paying too little attention to
traffic. Slow down, and cover the brake pedal with your foot.

Now watch out for that man who has just bought an evening paper from the newsvendor on the corner. He is ambling absent-mindedly towards the kerb with his head buried behind the paper, his mind occupied, as like as not, with the success of his football-pool coupon. Give him a wide berth. There's a driver in front who looks uncertain which direction to take. He's in the outside lane at the crossroads as though he were turning right, but he's peering out to look for the street name on the left-hand side. He may change his mind suddenly, so be prepared for it. You get a whiff of hot tar in your nostrils which warns you that roadworks are in progress somewhere near. Be ready to move into single-line traffic past the obstruction. A change of pitch in the vibration from the road wheels tells you that the road surface has changed. Is it the smooth type which will cause you to skid more easily if you have to pull up abruptly? Did that faint "peep" of a motor horn come from a road which crosses yours a little way ahead, or was it from traffic behind you? You can't be sure, but your reflexes are conditioned to anticipate the action necessary if it *is* a car coming from the side.

These are only some of the more obvious examples of road sense in action. In practice, all the incidents we have quoted might happen simultaneously. That marvellous mechanism, your brain, is quite capable of absorbing all this information in a fraction of a second and translating it into instructions to your limbs. Your job is to cultivate your power of perception so that it is kept informed in the minutest detail of what is going on around you, and this in turn will ensure that you are never taken by surprise.

Good-Mannered Driving

Good driving is *good-mannered* driving, and your mental attitude towards others will have an important bearing on your behaviour on the road. It is a sad truth that all too many otherwise delightful people seem to leave their natural courtesy behind when they get behind a steering wheel. It is not that they have any deliberate intention of being boorish to other road users: they simply do not carry over to their driving the discipline and the standards of reasonable conduct which they have been trained from their earliest years to observe in their everyday behaviour. Psychologists tell us that it is something to do with being cut off from the outside world in a box-on-wheels which gives us a sense of apartness. Whatever may be the reason, it is up to every driver to show tolerance and consideration for others, and to train himself to do so at all times and in all circumstances.

Some other driver or a pedestrian may display gross bad manners towards you, by cutting-in or by failing to dip his headlights at night, for instance, or by marching out into the road without warning. It doesn't help matters if you retaliate with equal bad manners—two wrongs only add up to danger on the road. Do not allow yourself to get irritated: with a mind which is full of resentment and annoyance, you are unable to concentrate on the job in hand.

Where pedestrians are concerned, bear in mind that they are much more exposed and vulnerable than you are, and they cannot move so quickly. When the weather is cold and wet, for example, they have an uncomfortable time of it waiting for a gap in a stream of heavy traffic before they can cross the road. You, on the other hand, are comfortably ensconced in a warm, dry motor car and it costs you only the not-very-considerable trouble of braking and starting off again to allow them to pass. How many times have *you* waited by the side of the road, getting miserably drenched, until some decent type in a car has stopped to make way for you? Remember that on wet roads your wheels will cause a good deal of splashing when they pass through deep puddles. If it is safe to do so, pull out so that you do not spray muddy water on to passers-by; otherwise, slow down so that your wheels do not throw up water.

Use your horn intelligently. If you approach another road user who shows no sign of being aware of your presence, give a gentle toot on your horn to warn him. A loud, prolonged blast may make him start and precipitate him into doing something unexpected. On the other hand when you want to overtake a large, noisy lorry, sound your horn firmly to make sure that the driver can hear it above the roar of his engine.

On a narrow hill in a country district, give way to vehicles coming up if you are descending. It is much easier for you to stop and start off again on a downward slope than it is for the other driver to perform a hill-start, as you will know from your own experience.

In all your actions on the road, try to imagine the difficulties of others, and do what you can to prevent or alleviate them. There are bound to be occasions when, having indicated that you are about to make a turn in one direction, you realize that you have made a mistake. If you have consideration for others, it will go completely against the grain to make a sudden swerve in an effort to retrieve your error, thus endangering those around you. The instinct resulting from your training in expert hands will prevent you from performing any *bêtise* of this kind. Depending on the circumstances, you can do one of two things. You can either make it clear to other drivers that you have changed your mind, and hold them up while you re-position your car, or you can accept the consequences of your own mistakes by carrying on in the direction that you originally indicated, with the intention of finding a drive or side-road in which to reverse. There are no prizes for the reader who selects the right answer.

You will learn, in practice, to avoid unnecessary signalling by so positioning your car that your intentions are unmistakeable to other drivers. You will be ready to dispense with the invariable use of signals, however, only when your use of the mirror is so habitual and your road sense is so developed that you are completely master of your driving.

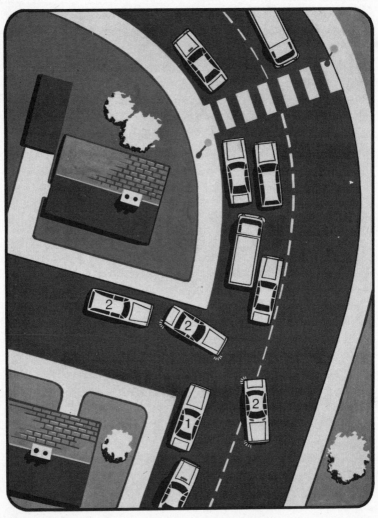

When travelling in a long line of traffic always leave a space (Car 1) for traffic to emerge from your left (Cars 2).

Courtesy breeds courtesy and there are many more considerate drivers on the roads than bad-mannered ones. Never
assume, however, that "the other man" will show the same
consideration towards you that you are prepared to extend to
him. He may have had a quarrel with his wife, or a ticking-off
from his boss. He may be preoccupied through any number of
reasons. He may be just plain stupid or he may be a rude and
aggressive type anyway. Let him go. His room is preferable to
his company and the greater the distance he puts between you,
the safer it will be. It is amazing, too, how often you will find
that the man who shaved past you and cut dangerously across
your path at the start of a journey, and whose progress up the
road was punctuated by fierce braking, vicious acceleration,
tail-hugging, swerving acceleration and similar offences against
good driving, will be seen only a few car-lengths ahead when
you come to traffic lights or a hold-up some miles farther on.
He risked his own life and the lives of others a dozen times in
the course of a few miles—for what? For the sake of several
dozen yards' advance in the traffic stream. Profit by his bad
example, for "Manners maketh the Motorist".

16

———

Taking the Test

During the weeks while you have been advancing in knowledge and experience, the prospect of taking the test will have
loomed larger and larger in your mind. Very probably you will
have heard a great deal of arrant nonsense talked about it.
Most learners have to suffer dark hints of bribery and corrup-
tion, knowing stories about trick questions from the examiners.
Take no notice of them whatever. The test is perfectly straightforward, with no traps and no jiggery-pokery. All you have to
do is to show the examiner that you can handle your car with
safety and with consideration for others, and that you are
thoroughly conversant with the rules of the Highway Code.

If your instructor thinks that you are not yet ready for the
test, he will tell you so and you would be wise to heed his
advice. Failure to pass the test the first time is no disgrace, but
it can be a setback to your confidence which you can do without. Apart from the fact that you will have spent the £3·25 fee
to no avail, you will have taken a place in the queue of someone
who is fit to pass and so lengthened the waiting list, which in
some parts of the country is long enough already.

Let us assume that you have absorbed all the instructions
and advice we have given you in this book, and that you are
competent to carry them out without fuss or fumble. In that
case you are indeed fit to take the test, and you should pass
without any difficulty at all. When you took out your provisional licence you were given a little pamplet issued by the
Ministry of Transport and numbered "D.L.68". Like hundreds
of others, you probably gave it a cursory glance and threw it

into a drawer. Take it out now and read it carefully. It contains some valuable advice for those intending to take the test.

"Examination nerves" affect some people more than others but most people suffer from them in some degree. When the time comes for the examiner to climb into the passenger seat, pencil and notepad at the ready, acute sufferers are already in an advanced state of jitters and they often put up a lamentable performance, which does not in the least reflect their actual abilities. Examiners are understanding men who appreciate from their daily experience that the tension of the test can be extremely painful for some, and a mistake which is obviously the result of pure nerves is not going to disqualify you provided the examiner is satisfied that you are in fact on top of your driving. However, it is not a bad idea to get used to the atmosphere of the test by carrying out one or more "dummy runs" in advance. Your instructor should take you over a typical "test run" and behave as though he were in fact the examiner, with a pad on which he notes down your success or failure to perform properly the manoeuvres he dictates.

The object of the test is to satisfy the authorities that you are fit to be given a licence to drive your car unaccompanied and in all conditions of traffic. Showy driving will get you nowhere, and will indicate to your examiner that you are in a state of over-confidence which must be corrected. If you take a sharp bend in a controlled slide which would be the envy of a top-class racing driver, your examiner is not going to be impressed (he will probably be scared to death), but if he asks you "what was the sign we have just passed?" and you are unable to give him the right answer, then you will have earned a black mark.

Given expert training, there should not be any need to "mug up" the Highway Code because you will have been quizzed on this many times right from your first driving lesson. It may be, however, that you have not had actual experience of putting into practice some of the rules it contains—motorway driving, for example, is forbidden to learners. You are still expected to be thoroughly familiar with everything in the Code and must be prepared to answer questions on any part of it. That applies equally to the sections devoted to "The Road-User on Foot" and "The Road-User and Animals".

While you have been under instruction you will have been prompted from time to time as to the next move. Your teacher will have pointed out the signs as you approach them and will have told you what sequence of movements to adopt in order to prepare for the next manoeuvre. You will get none of this help in the test. You are on your own. If the test is to be conducted in a district with which you are unfamiliar, it is *not* cheating to take some trouble exploring it so that you will not be nonplussed by some particularly complicated road layout. Even if you have no opportunity to do this, it does not matter, because the examiner will give you plenty of notice when he wants you to turn left or right and the conditions, after all, will be no different from those you will experience when you have gained your full licence. When that time comes, you will have to rely on your own judgement without even this assistance.

Let us imagine that you are about to set out on the test. The examiner has exchanged a few words of ordinary conversation with you to put you at your ease.

Now he tells you to move off and to get ready to take the first turning on the right. First, glance over shoulder and look in your mirror, signal if necessary when the road is clear behind you, and off you go with a nice, smooth display of clutch-control, moving up without jerky changes into top gear. There's the "road junction" sign a little way ahead. Mirror. Nothing coming behind, so move over to the crown of the road. Change down in good time, and stop at the mouth of the turning, your front wheels at a slight angle, to allow on-coming traffic to go through. A cyclist has moved up on your near side. He obviously intends to take the right-hand turning, too. Let him go first, waiting until he is well clear before you begin to follow, in case he swerves.

This is a quiet, residential road and there is very little other traffic, but that milkman who has walked out of a gateway marking an entry in his accounts book doesn't show any sign of having heard you coming. Give him a gentle toot on the horn to make sure. What was that sign we just passed? "A school sign". This is just about finishing time for schools, so watch out for children round the next bend. You can see the school entrance some way off because a white-coated school crossing warden is standing there, with a cluster of youngsters behind the safety railings. The warden is clearly about to hold up the traffic because she is lifting her notice board into the "ready" position. Slow down and change down so that you do not have to brake sharply with a squealing of tyres.

You have just passed a "Give Way" sign and the examiner wants you to turn right again. Mirror, signal and take up the correct positioning. When you reach the stop line make sure that your wheels do in fact stop turning. This road is busier, so wait until there is a good safe gap in the traffic before you move, with a quick look right, left and right again at the last minute just to be quite certain. The examiner is making a note on his pad. Did you do something wrong? It does not necessarily follow, because he reports the good as well as the bad. In any case, it's too late to worry now about what is past. The important thing is to do your best during the remainder of the examination. Unless you do something which is a blatant show of bad manners or you patently cannot control the vehicle properly, a single mistake will not result in your being "ploughed". Anyway, never dwell on your mistakes.

Your route takes you through congested streets and you have to show that you know how to overtake parked or moving vehicles, that you are alert to obey road signs or the directions of a policeman, that you have been correctly taught to take corners neither too wide nor too sharply, that you show courtesy to pedestrians and other road users, that you can take roundabouts in your stride—that you are capable, in fact, of negotiating in safety any of the obstacles and hazards which are to be found in a typical built-up area. At all times you will be meticulous in giving signals for the benefit of others, and you will use your mirror constantly so that you know what is happening behind you.

If, during the course of the test, a dog runs suddenly under your wheels and you have to perform an emergency stop in order to avoid it, it is unlikely that the examiner will ask you to do it again. He will be satisfied already that you know how to behave in an emergency. An emergency stop is, however, a routine part of the test and it is considerably less unnerving to be asked to do it in a quiet side-street in the knowledge that there is nothing coming up behind. The examiner does not suddenly call on you to make an emergency stop without warning. He tells you that this is the next manoeuvre he wants you to perform, and explains that he will not ask you to do it until he has made sure that it is safe. The usual signal given is a tap on the windscreen or facia panel with his notebook. It is then up to you to show that you can move like lightning when the need arises.

You will also be required to demonstrate your ability to drive the car backwards and steer it into a limited opening. Again, a side street is usually chosen for this and you must show that you can reverse round the corner without cutting too close to the pavement and without swinging the bonnet too far out into the road you are leaving. You must also finish up with your wheels reasonably close to the kerb.

Another exercise in reversing will come when you are told to turn the vehicle round in the road so that you are facing in the direction you have come. It is not true that the examiners choose the road with the steepest camber they can find for this test. If you *do* have to do it on a sharply-cambered road, however, treat it as a challenge, and make sure that your wheels do not touch the kerb on either side. Remember, too, that you are not obliged to make a "three-point turn". You can make as many forward and reverse movements as you like, within reason, and it depends on the length of the car you are driving and the width of the road whether you can manage it in three or not.

When you get back to the examination centre, the examiner will ask you some straightforward questions to test your knowledge of the Highway Code. It is best if you can quote the relevant rule word for word, but you will not be failed providing you can express the sense of the paragraph fully and accurately. If stuck just imagine you are in the driving seat and then tell the examiner what you would do. Also during the Test he will ask you to read the number-plate of a car some distance away to prove that you are able, as you testified in your application for a licence, to do this at a distance of 75 feet in the case of symbols $3\frac{1}{2}''$ high or 67 feet in the case of symbols $3\frac{1}{8}''$ high.

That is all there is to it. The order of the events we have described here may not be the same, but the content of the test does not vary. No tricks, no traps, and perfectly fair.

It does not surprise us in the least, to learn that YOU HAVE PASSED! If not, don't worry, study the faults enumerated on your "Statement of Failure", understand, accept and rectify them. Then try again.

17

You're on Your Own

Your 'prentice days are done; the freedom of the Queen's Highway is yours. Without "L" plates to advertise your novitiate, you no longer feel that all the world and his family of small, staring schoolboys are enjoying the free spectacle of your red-faced embarrassment when you stall the engine or crash the gears. Oddly enough, mistakes of that kind seem to be much less frequent the moment you are able to remove those badges of your inexpertise. But do not forget that the possession of a licence to drive a car unaccompanied does not automatically make you into an experienced driver. It proclaims merely that you have been able to satisfy the licensing authority that you have mastered the basic principles. There is still a lot to be learnt and, if you are a conscientious driver, you will never stop learning.

Without the reassuring presence of your instructor beside you, it is in the natural order of things that you should suffer the fluttering of butterflies in your stomach on your first solo run. For the first time, perhaps you come to the full realization of the tremendous responsibility you carry when you are navigating a ton of metal-on-wheels through the obstacle-course of a busy traffic scene. Without your "L" plates you are on equal terms with drivers, cyclists and pedestrians who have no reason to suppose that you are any less competent than the most expert among them. They will not make allowances for you as they did while you were under tuition. Without prompting of any kind, you must form your own judgements and make your own decisions to cope with conditions as you find them.

Equally, you must not suppose that everyone else on the road will react in precisely the same way as you would do to a given situation. Never assume that the other man will behave in a certain set of circumstances as you would do in his place. It is nothing more than mental arrogance to take the line: "I am right and the other man is a fool". He may well be thinking the same about you. If an accident results it is no great comfort to be upheld in a magistrate's court. At best you will have to pay the amount of the "excess" clause in your insurance policy to foot the garage bill, and will lose your "no-claim" bonus to boot; at worst the accident could result in injuries to yourself and/or your passengers. Like the brilliant repartee which only comes to you when a conversation is over and you are going over it in retrospect, it is too late to think after an accident of how you could have avoided it. Make allowances, therefore, for other drivers to commit errors either of omission or of commission and add to this with an extra margin to cover any mistakes you may make yourself. Care may "cost" a few seconds, but it does help to prevent accidents.

When you are labouring up a steep hill, for example, and you see that you will have to pull out into the path of oncoming traffic to pass a stationary car, it would be foolishness to take it for granted that vehicles descending will give you precedence, as you have been taught to do in a case like this. Nine times out of ten, the man coming down will make way for you by slowing down and giving the appropriate hand signal to let you (and others behind him) know that he is doing so. The tenth man, however, having just got the worst of an argument with somebody or other will be in the mood to assert himself, and you will come seriously unstuck if you try to tangle with him.

Practice Makes Experience

It will not be long before you begin to learn some of the "tricks of the trade" which enable you to get about, especially in towns, more easily and with greater safety. Drivers who regularly travel between two points usually experiment with different routes to find the one which skirts places where congestion is frequent and thus avoids the boredom of bumper-to-bumper crawling and the stink of exhaust fumes. At some point or other, it is almost invariably necessary to cross a main road. When this happens, it is commonsense to choose an intersection which is controlled by traffic lights or by a point-duty policeman. It is difficult and can be dangerous to try to edge out of a side-road into a heavy stream of traffic. If this procedure is not practicable, then it is preferable to pick your route so that you enter the main road by a left-hand turning which takes you *with* the stream of traffic. You complete the crossing by taking a right turn later on. Some crossroads are "staggered" in this way deliberately. The purpose is to reduce the danger-potential by dividing it— drivers have fewer hazards to contend with at each point.

As you become more "traffic-wise" you will learn, too, that there are occasions when it would not be feasible to drive in strict accordance with the book. You have had it drummed into your mind, for instance, that you should keep to the left-hand lane in traffic unless you plan to take a right turn or unless there is ample room for two lines abreast. If remaining in the left-hand lane means that you continually have to edge out into the other lane to overtake stationary vehicles, you will be placing yourself unnecessarily "at risk" each time, to the irritation of other drivers, and may even find yourself balked altogether until someone in the outside lane is kind enough to let you out. Commonsense dictates that it is safer to stay in single file, moving at a steady pace, than to keep popping in and out like a jack-in-the-box.

We have been speaking here about busy town conditions. On a dual-carriageway built to take three lanes of traffic in each direction, you should similarly keep to the inside lane as much as you can, but if there is a procession of slow traffic on the kerb side it is bad practice to keep weaving backwards and forwards. In that case, use the middle lane until the inside lane is clear for a reasonable distance ahead. This does *not* apply, however, to a road with only three lanes to accommodate traffic in both directions. On these the centre lane is very dangerous territory indeed. Be especially careful when overtaking that there is nothing coming towards you which is either overtaking or likely to overtake before you can get back to your near side. And try to avoid overtaking in such a way that when you are passing one vehicle another vehicle coming the other way is abreast of you at the same time.

Motorway Driving

Lane discipline is even more important, if that be possible, when you are driving on a motorway, which, as a fully-fledged driver you are now entitled to do. The main reason why motorways have proved to be so much safer than other roads is that different classes of road-user are segregated and there are no hazards such as crossroads, traffic lights, sharp bends, roundabouts or junctions. You should find no pedestrians, animals, cyclists, mo-peds, learner-drivers, invalid carriages or agricultural vehicles (although you should always be prepared for the unexpected—a pack of hounds in full cry after a fox once dashed across the London-Birmingham motorway, to the no small consternation of drivers). Motorways are not race-tracks, but they are engineered specifically for speed with safety. The rules do not differ greatly from those applying on ordinary roads but because everything is happening so much more quickly it is vital that they should be obeyed to the letter. Never move from one lane to another without first checking carefully in your mirror to see that there is nothing coming up behind you and preparing to overtake. Bear in mind that the car which shows as a mere speck in the mirror may be travelling at anything up to, or even over, 70 m.p.h. and will overhaul you in much less time than you may expect. Before changing lanes, signal your intention well in advance and move back to the lane you have left as soon as you can do so safely. As on ordinary twin-track roads, keep to the nearside lane unless this involves constantly pulling out to pass slower vehicles, in which case, remain in the centre lane.

Direction signs on motorways give you plenty of advance warning of an exit point. If you propose to turn off, start reducing speed as soon as you see the first sign and get into the left-hand lane. If, for some reason, you realize that you should have turned off when you have already passed the slip road, there is nothing for it but to carry on until you come to the next exit. It would be madness, as well as illegal, to try reversing.

Resist any temptation to drive "flat out" (anyway the maximum speed limit at present is 70 m.p.h.)—your car is not used to it and if you keep it up for any length of time the engine will be subjected to stresses from which it may never recover. It is also kinder to the engine to close the throttle occasionally by easing your foot off the gas pedal. Your speed will not vary appreciably and in any event you will achieve better petrol consumption.

Talking of petrol consumption, do not forget that at higher speeds your tank will empty much faster. See that you have enough to get you at least as far as the next service station. If you do run out, you will have to pull on to the hard shoulder on the left and walk to the nearest telephone post—these are sited at intervals of one mile and are connected with the police. If you are a member, the A.A., called by the police, will bring you some petrol and you will have suffered no more than inconvenience. If you do not belong to a motoring organization, the police will call a garage for you and your petrol will cost you dear because you will have to pay for the outward and return mileage of the breakdown vehicle which may have to make a round trip of thirty miles or so to reach you.

High winds can be dangerous when you are travelling at speed, particularly if there are strong gusts. These can have a marked effect on the steering. If you get a nasty sensation as though you are floating on air, the reason is that the car is trying to do just that. The remedy is to reduce speed. By the same token, heavy rain should be treated with respect. At very high speeds the car may begin to "aqua-plane" on the surface of water which cannot drain away quickly enough, and as it is not equipped with a rudder the steering will be non-existent. Again, reduce speed. In any case you should travel more slowly in rain, on the motorway as on other roads, because of the increased danger of skidding. Moreover you cannot see properly if you are going so fast that the wipers are unable to give you a constant clear view of the road ahead.

When you leave the motorway and mingle with traffic on the ordinary road system, remember that it takes a little time to adjust yourself to the changed conditions. After a steady 50, 60 or 70 m.p.h., 30 m.p.h. seems little more than walking pace.

We have mentioned only some of the more important rules of motorway driving here in order to emphasize the vital necessity to observe lane discipline. Before ever venturing on to a motorway, however, you would be well advised to refresh your memory of the "Motorway Driving" section of the Highway Code. Make sure that you are thoroughly conversant with all the advice it contains, and put all of it into practice.

And Finally . . .

There seem to be an awful lot of "Do's" and "Don't's" about driving, you may think. "Remember this", "Don't forget about that"—this book is literally peppered with injunctions and adjurations. This is in the nature of teaching, whatever the subject may be. When the "Do's" and "Don't's" have become part of your natural driving habit they will not appear in the least formidable. On the contrary, you will get a great deal of enjoyment and satisfaction from doing the job properly and doing it well. We hope this book will have helped you to take that modest pride in your driving which reaps its own reward in terms of better, safer motoring today.

18

Tuition for the Disabled

We have dealt with the tuition and progress of the physically and mentally capable would-be driver. Obviously, anyone who is mentally incapable should not even think of driving a car; quite different, however, is the case of the physically-disabled potential driver.

There are thousands of disabled motorists and would-be motorists in the United Kingdom and throughout most countries. Some are war veterans, suffering from the after-effects of wounds or loss of limbs; others are victims of paralysis, arthritis, deformities and disabling accidents of all kinds.

The introduction of the motorized invalid carriage has made it possible for many of these people to become mobile. But what about the vast number who want to drive a normal car, to have the opportunity of driving their families just like any other motorist and to take their proper place on the roads today? The same standard of passing the Ministry of Transport test is required from them as from anyone else. The authors can say unhesitatingly from personal experience that, through modifications to car controls and specialized driving tuition, almost every disablement can be overcome and the incapacitated motorist can take his place on the highway on equal terms.

The Ministry of Transport has created special tests and today the examination for the disabled motorist extends considerably further than the standard test. Obviously the driver must conform to the basic principles laid down by the Ministry in operating the car and its controls completely and safely, though in some cases—and a sign fitted to the back of the car informs other drivers of the fact—hand signals can be omitted.

Tuition, then, provided the necessary controls adjustments have been made and a qualified instructor is employed, is the same as has already been outlined in the preceding chapters. But how does the incapacitated driver first start going about taking on the problem of driving his or her orthodox car?

Initially, a check-test should take place, to assess the extent of disability and the individual requirements of the would-be driver. The B.S.M., which has created so many car adaptations for the physically disabled, has a special Disability Test Chassis, built at its own workshops. On this machine, each of the controls—steering, clutch, gear lever, foot and hand brakes—are interconnected with instruments, the recordings of which enable an assessment to be made of the work effort available from each limb.

One of the most important safety factors in driving a car is to ensure that the seating is arranged to provide complete ease of operation of all the controls, wherever they may be positioned. The pupil suffering from a weakness of the arms becomes an efficient motorist when the seating is so raised that his arms can relax downwards towards the steering wheel. So with leg disabilities—a small adaptation of clutch cradle or a cradle covering the brake pedal, coupled with a hydraulic booster, ensures complete control with a hand throttle.

On the test machine, the seat is adjustable both horizontally and vertically, so that the exact requirement can be discovered. The handbrake is duplicated for both central and right-hand operation. The gear lever is also duplicated by central and steering-column control. Each potential driver's reaction time is calibrated by a special time clock which records in 1/20th seconds. Each pupil tested is provided with a certificate containing all these essential details. This machine, unique in this country and perhaps in the world, has already enabled the adaptation requirements of many hundreds of physically incapacitated drivers to be assessed, thus enabling them to go on and become proficient motorists.

What sort of disabilities can be overcome and by what means? Special instruments are designed to reduce a handicap. Simple to handle, and often detachable, these are used during tuition and can be transferred to the drivers' own cars. Modifications can be designed to fit in with the normal arrangement of controls and therefore do not confine a car's use to the disabled driver.

With the increasing number of cars fitted with automatic transmission, less adaptations will probably be necessary— and anyway, in most cases, adaptations are inexpensive to remove so that a car can be restored to its original condition in the event of re-sale.

When the feet and legs cannot be used, all controls are hand-operated. Hand-controlled clutch and throttle levers, fitted under the steering wheels, can be operated by the fingers of one hand without removing it from the steering wheel. These controls have a light, easy action. Finger-grip control is essential, for while the left hand copes with the gear lever or hand-operated "foot" brake, the right must steer and release the clutch. Another hand-controlled clutch is worked by a trigger on the gear lever, which allows the clutch to be released and the gear change made in one movement of one hand.

Leg disability is only part of the story, however. For a driver with no hands, special equipment has been designed in the form of a superimposed steering wheel and gimbal rings fitted to the gear lever and handbrake, together with various adaptations created to ensure complete operation of the controls.

Many people suffer from left-arm disabilities. Here, a right-hand gear change conversion is possible, appropriate to most cars with a central gear change and, where necessary, the hand-brake can similarly be transferred to the right. By these means it is possible to have complete control of the steering wheel, changing gear as and when necessary, it being an essential requirement of the Ministry test that the driver should maintain contact with the steering wheel at all times. In cases where this may not be possible with the hand alone, there is a steering wheel damper—by which means the steering can be held steady by the knee, so controlling the steering when travelling in a straight line (when all gear-changing sequences should take place).

For the driver who has lost an arm, an extension of the gear lever by a detachable lever is possible, while a rotary hand-grip steering ball—used for sharp corners and full-lock turns —can be attached to the steering wheel.

An artificial arm can in many cases be used for normal steering with the help of a ball and socket steering aid. Rotary steering balls are attached to the steering wheel (as many as the driver requires) and a small, light socket which fits over them screws easily into the driver's artificial hand or arm appliance. This gives complete steering control and can even be used with greater speed on a full-lock turn or sharp corner than the two-handed turn of a physically capable person. Adaptations shaped to fit the artificial hand can also be used on the gear lever and handbrake.

These are just some of the methods by which disability can be overcome when driving the normal modern car. We could go on explaining further means—but that would almost be a book on its own.

Our experience over many years is that the disabled driver is a competent and safe motorist. This is backed up by the very competitive rates which they normally receive from insurance companies and the number of outstandingly good drivers to be found among members of the Disabled Drivers' Motor Club.

The main lesson to be derived from this chapter is that if you are unfortunate enough to suffer physical disability, don't be discouraged. Do go to a fully-qualified specialist in the field of driving adaptations for the incapacitated and do go to a driving school where the instructors are capable of giving the necessary specialized tuition. From our own knowledge we can tell you that only two per cent of the disabled would-be drivers who have applied for guidance at the B.S.M., for instance, have had to be turned away.

And, above all, don't forget the lessons to be learned from the preceding chapters in this book—they apply as much to you as to anyone else who appreciates that good driving pays.

19

The Law and Your Car

The growth of motoring has brought in its train a whole welter of legislation affecting car ownership and use. Hardly a week goes by without some new regulation, or an amendment to an existing regulation, being introduced. It would be absurd to expect ordinary people to know and understand all these laws: even the best legal brains are sometimes baffled over the interpretation of ambiguous or obscure passages, particularly when it comes to applying, for example, some of the clauses of the Highway Act of 1835 which is still in force today. Yet the basis of British justice is the supposition that every citizen knows the law: hence the well-worn expression that "the law is an ass!"

Ass or not, you are now bound to comply with thousands of "Do's" and "Don't's"—yes, more of them!—contained in thousands of distinctly dusty pieces of reading within covers bearing exciting titles such as "The Road Vehicles Lighting (Standing Vehicles) (Exemption) Regulations, 1955 and 1956" or, an even more efficacious cure for insomnia, the "Motor Vehicles (Speed Limits on Special Roads) Regulations, 1959." You could read solidly for a month and still not get to the end of them.

When all is said and done, however, the law is only a set of rules made by man for the benefit of society and at the root of all the legal mumbo-jumbo is a commonsense code of conduct without which we should soon find ourselves in a pretty pickle. Put out of your mind any thought that you have now joined a persecuted and under-privileged section of the community, as some people will have you believe. There are plenty of restrictions, yes, but they are sensible ones, based on the reasonable rights of everyone, and the roads would be safer places if all road users obeyed them implicitly. Aside from the technical complexities of phraseology, which are best left to the lawyers anyway, it is not difficult to master the major points of the law which you need to know for safety on the roads. They are given in outline in the section of the Highway Code headed "The Law's Demands" and we propose here to do no more than to elaborate some of the more important of them.

Vehicle Licence

Before a car is driven on the roads, it must be registered with the Licensing Authority, who will allocate to it the combination of letters and numbers—the registration number—which it will carry throughout its life. This registration number must be displayed on the front and rear of the car in white characters* of given dimensions and spacing on a black background, the number plate to be completely flat and vertical. Owners of low-slung sports cars have been known to remove the front number plate in the belief that it affected the aerodynamics of the vehicle, and have painted the registration number on the sloping bonnet instead.

When the vehicle is first registered, a Registration Book, more commonly known as the Log Book, is issued. This is in effect the car's identity card and in it are entered details of its "life"—its changes of ownership, licence renewals, changes of

* Motor vehicles in this country may now use reflective number plates. They can be fitted at either end of a vehicle or at both ends according to choice. The important difference between a front and back plate is that a front plate must consist of black digits on a white reflective background, while a back plate must consist of black digits on a yellow background.

colour or construction, and so on. Keep it in a safe place and do not forget, if you change your address, that the Licensing Authority also wants to know, and to record in the Log Book, the car has "moved home". If you sell the car, the Log Book goes with it. If you buy a car you also take possession of its Registration Book. Possession of the Log Book, however, is not proof of ownership—a point to remember especially if you buy a used vehicle from a dealer of whose integrity you have no knowledge.

The Vehicle Licence—still often referred to as the Road Fund Licence, long after the Road Fund as such has ceased to exist—is issued by the Licensing Authority of the district in which you live, who also issue your driving licence. The Vehicle Licence costs £25 annually for all cars irrespective of engine capacity, with the exception (it is always the exceptions which makes the law so complicated) of certain small cars first registered before 1 January 1947. It takes the form of a small circular disc and the law has a good deal to say about the way it must be displayed on your vehicle. Vehicle manufacturers usually save you the trouble of swotting up the regulations on this point by providing a licence holder on the left-hand side of the windscreen in a position which complies with the legal requirements.

You do not have to take out a vehicle licence for a whole year at a time if you don't want to. Nor do you need to take it out on 1 January so that it runs for the calendar year. Licences are issued or renewed for any period of four months or for twelve months from the beginning of any month, if you know what we mean! Read the sentence twice, slowly and you will have saved yourself several pages of close print in the relevant Regulation.

Whenever a car is sold and the Registration Book is handed to the new owner, the change of ownership must be notified by the seller to the Licensing Authority and the new owner must send the book to the Authority, with his name and address duly entered in it. If you lose the Log Book or if it becomes defaced, you can get a new one on payment of 25p.

Insurance

One of the most serious offences in the motoring calendar is to drive while uninsured. To comply with Act of Parliament you must be covered for "third party" risks, that is, claims made by a third party for death or personal injuries caused by or arising from the use of the vehicle on the road. The ordinary motorist is not obliged to take out insurance cover in respect of passengers. The insurance company issues you with a certificate which it is advisable to carry with you. Most people tuck it inside their driving licences. The insurance certificate must be obtained and produced if demanded by a policeman; if you are not carrying it with you, you must produce it at a police station, which you have nominated, within five clear days.

Read your insurance policy carefully. Some policies expressly state "driver only", in which case your policy is inoperative if someone else drives your car. Similarly, if a friend offers to let you drive his car, you must be sure that the insurance for that car is in order.

Always renew your insurance before the due date. The insurance company will send you a reminder well before it expires and it is folly to slip this in a drawer where it can so easily be forgotten. Make out the cheque straight away and send it off.

The insurance comes to an end when a car is sold unless the insurers agree to assign the contract of insurance to the new owner.

Driving Licence

A full driving licence can be obtained only after passing the

Ministry of Transport driving examination. It costs £1 and lasts for three years, and it must be signed, in ink, by the person to whom it is issued. Failure to do this lays you open to a fine up to £5. If you let it lapse for ten years you will have to pass the test again, whether you have done so before or not.

Beginners have to take out a provisional licence, which is valid for twelve months and costs £1. It entitles a learner driver to handle the car only when accompanied by a supervisor, who must be a person who has passed the driving test himself, holds a licence (not being a provisional licence), or who has held a full licence for at least two years. "L" plates must be carried at front and rear, the colours and dimensions of which are exactly specified in the regulations. You can rely on proprietary plates bought from a reputable shop conforming to the law. Section 102 (4) of the Road Traffic Act 1960 deals with provisional licences and how long a motorist can drive with such a licence. It is couched in general terms but sets out the principle that there must be a 12 months' limit to the time a motorist can drive without taking the Ministry test. But the section has also an escape clause—reasonable excuse for not having taken the Ministry test. Reasonable cause can be interpreted to cover the slow learner who has little aptitude for driving and needs many hours of tuition and practice before becoming a competent and safe motorist.

Fitness to Drive

There is no health test for drivers in Britain, as there is in some countries abroad. The Licensing Authority, however, has power to revoke a licence if they have reason to believe that the licence-holder is suffering from some disease or physical disability which will seriously impair his control of a vehicle, to the danger of other road-users.

Everyone knows that it is a serious offence, punishable by heavy fines and/or imprisonment, plus disqualification from driving, to be in charge of a car while under the influence of drink or drugs. Drunken driving rightly carries with it a social stigma in proportion to the gravity of the offence. But remember that medical evidence has proved beyond any shadow of doubt that alcohol, even in quite small amounts, has an effect on your driving. One small drink, therefore, while it will not by any means make you drunk, will affect your fitness to drive. Don't mix the two. Remember as well that fatigue also causes a "fall-off" in one's ability.

Breathalyser Law

The old law relating to being in charge of a motor vehicle while under the influence of drink or drugs, is still in force. However, with the breathalyser law, you will be committing an offence if, while in charge of a motor vehicle, the level of alcohol in your blood is more than 80 milligrams per 100 millilitres, with an equivalent for urine of 107 milligrams per 100 millilitres. You have been warned.

Vehicle Roadworthiness

It's not much use being as fit as a fiddle and as competent a driver as they come if your vehicle is not in a roadworthy condition. Brakes, steering, lights and tyres—these are the four vitally important aspects which call for special care. Constant checking is necessary to make sure that they are always in good condition—and the law will come down on you like a ton of bricks if they are found to be defective. At the moment all vehicles which have been registered for 3 years or more must have an annual inspection and receive a Ministry of Transport Certificate of Roadworthiness.

The golden rule that you must have unhindered vision is enshrined in the regulations which say that your windscreen must be kept clean and that the windscreen wiper (it is not obligatory to have two) must be in working order.

Your tyres must be in sound condition. It is now an offence if a tyre does not have a tread pattern at least 1 mm. deep in a continuous band of pattern at least three-quarters of the tread width. It is also an offence if the type is unsuitable either in itself or in combination with other tyres on the vehicle; not properly inflated; or has a break in its fabric or a serious cut, a lump or bulge caused by ply separation or failure, or any portion of the ply structure exposed.

Considering the importance of the rear-view mirror, the law is singularly vague about its fitting and adjustment. What it says is that "every motor vehicle shall be equipped either internally or externally with a mirror so constructed and fitted to the motor vehicle as to assist the driver if he so desires to become aware of traffic to the rear of the vehicle and on both sides rearward". The message is clear, however, and it is worth pointing out here that if the rear window of a car is obstructed by luggage, an internal mirror is not "so constructed and fitted . . ." (as above!)

Your car must be fitted with a "warning instrument" which is "capable of giving audible and sufficient warning of its approach or position". Usually, this is the electric horn, but if you have a hankering for one of the old-fashioned bulb horns, there is nothing against it. Your "warning instrument" must not, however, be a gong or a bell or a siren: these are reserved for fire, police and ambulance service. You must not sound your horn while stationary, or between 11.30 p.m. and 7 a.m. in built-up areas.

It is an offence to drive a car which is unduly noisy and it must not emit "smoke, vapour, grit, sparks, ashes, cinders or oily substance" if damage, injury or danger is caused or likely to be caused.

To comply with the regulations, you must have two white obligatory lights and two headlights showing to the front and two red lights *and* two reflectors showing to the rear. The law requires that these should be in efficient working order even in the daytime, when they may not be in use. This is only commonsense, however, since you may need to use them in fog. Your headlamps must be properly adjusted.

If you carry luggage or some other load on the outside of the car, it must not project beyond the width of your car to such an extent that it causes danger to other road users, and it must be securely fastened so that it is not likely to fall off into the road.

Nowadays there are varying speed limits—"differential speed limits" is the official term for them—and whether the signs indicate "30", "40", "50", "60" or "70" m.p.h. you must obey them, just as you must obey other regulatory signs such as the "Stop" or "Give Way", or the direction of a policeman.

Self-evidently, you must not drive recklessly or dangerously, without due care and attention or without reasonable consideration for others. If you have read this book thus far, you will need no further reminder on this point.

When you leave the car you must switch off the engine and apply the handbrake, and at night it is an offence to leave your headlamps on when stationary.

If You Have an Accident

If you are unlucky enough to be involved in an accident which involves personal injury to any person, even if it was not your fault; or which causes any damage to any vehicle (not necessarily a motor vehicle); or which causes damage or injury to an animal (which includes a horse, ass, mule, sheep, pig, goat, dog or cattle, but not a cat or poultry); you must: stop and, if requested to do so, give your name and address, together with the name and address of the owner of the vehicle if it is not yours, to "anyone having reasonable grounds for requiring them".

If there is nobody to whom you can give these particulars at the time, you must report the accident to the police within 24 hours.

If anyone is injured, report the accident to the police as soon as possible, and in any case within 24 hours. If required to do so you must produce your certificate of insurance to the police, either when reporting the accident or within five days at any police station specified by you when reporting.

It is obviously prudent to take the names and addresses of any witness to the accident and it is equally important not to make any statement on the spot which could be construed as admitting liability. This is explicitly stated in your insurance policy and could seriously jeopardize your position in any proceedings which may follow.

Accidents do not just happen, they are *caused*. If you put into practice the precepts we have outlined in this book, you will not only never be responsible for an accident yourself, but you will stand a good chance of avoiding, through your development of road sense, the accident which some other driver seems intent on producing.

In Conclusion

All motorists should consider joining the Automobile Association and accordingly benefit from their many efficient—and free—services.

The AA exclusively recommend the many services offered by the British School of Motoring, and AA Members can claim special reduced terms on all B.S.M. Courses, including the special AA/B.S.M. Advanced Course.

Index

Index

Road markings

ACROSS THE ROAD

Give way to traffic on major road

Give way to traffic in roundabout

Stop lines at STOP sign

Stop line at signals or police control

Warning of Give Way sign

Box Junction See page xxx

ON THE ROAD

Double white lines   Diagonal stripes   Lane markings

No crossing

No crossing solid line if nearer to driver than broken line

Do not enter marked area

Lane line   Centre line   Warning line